Helping Yourself with ACUPINEOLOGY

Helping Yourself with ACUPINEOLOGY

Re-edited by

VcToria Gray,
daughter of Geof Gray-Cobb

The Alternative Universe
Edmonton, Alberta, Canada

Helping Yourself with ACUPINEOLOGY

Copyright © 2019

ISBN: 978-1-9991283-0-2

First edition, 1980
Revised edition, July 2019

Re-edited by VcToria Gray,
daughter of Geof Gray-Cobb

All rights reserved. No part of this book may be reproduced in any form or by any means, without permission in writing from the publisher.

This book is a reference work based on research by the author Geof Gray-Cobb. Deceased May 12th 2009.

Reprinted and re-published by
The Alternative Universe
Edmonton, Alberta, Canada
www.alternativeuniverse.ca

Other books by Geof Gray-Cobb (AKA Frater Malak)

The Mystic Grimoire of Mighty Spells and Rituals – Here are the most superior Spells and powerful Rituals—the bare bones of magic—set down step-by-step in plain, clear English by Frater Malak. Re-published April 2019.
ISBN: 978-0-9812138-5-9

NAP: The Miracle of New Avatar Power – How the secrets of the ancients are able to bring to you the life you are looking for. Follow Geof Gray-Cobb and the knowledge he imparts to you from years of research. Re-published and released May 2019.
ISBN: 978-0-9812138-7-3

Secrets From Beyond the Pyramids – Based on his understanding of the awesome power of the Pyramids, Geof Gray-Cobb shows you how New Psychic Energy Power can quickly and easily transform your present existence into a life of deep and lasting satisfaction. To be re-published in November 2019.
ISBN: 978-1-9991283-1-9

Amazing Secrets of New Avatar Power – Your mind, body and soul run on New Avatar Power and so does the whole Universe. A follow up to his last New Avatar Power book originally released in 1974, this 1978 publication will be released in January 2020.
ISBN: 978-1-9991283-2-6

My Father's Original Dedication

In gratitude for the constant inspiration, stimulation and example of Darius, Harry, Louis, Peter, Timothy, O'Grady and all other karmic connections.

VcToria's Dedication

This book is dedicated to my 'favorite grandson Liam', who every time I would say that to him he would reply 'I am your only grandson, Grandma'. Then we would laugh. May we always laugh together, here or on the other side.

VcToria's Foreword

Advice: This book needs to be read from the beginning to end or you will not comprehend it properly. Once you have read through it, take a note book and create all the aspects of 'activation'. Only then begin your journey of change. You will thank me if you do this the correct way.

When reading the finger and hand placements read them VERY slowly and they will make perfect sense. If you wish to order the Figure One and Two from the book you may do so from the web store at: **www.alternativeuniverse.ca**

If you have arthritis or any type of finger stiffness that will not allow you to bend your fingers, you may obtain a crystal wand and use the point. This is to be done in situations where you absolutely cannot bend your fingers.

If you need help with the calculations in the last chapter please see VcToria's web store to purchase at **www.alternativeuniverse.ca**

INTRODUCTION:
HOW THIS BOOK CAN BRING YOU HAPPINESS, HEALTH, FREEDOM, AND MATERIAL SUCCESS

Every day you can see other people getting lucky. They win lotteries, get fabulous jobs, find their soul mates, snap from ill health to total fitness and energy, vanquish their enemies—they're able to forget about misery and poverty and sail serenely into a glorious future, free from the trials and tribulations which afflict so many others.

You can join those happy people, starting right now. Your dreams, no matter how hopeless they may seem at the moment, can come true, exactly as they have for the thousands of others you hear about on the radio, read about in the newspapers, or see on television.

With this book you can easily and automatically use your mind and body to draw life-changing influences to you—influences that have been around since this universe was created—so that you will receive your full and overflowing share of the luck, happiness, and fulfillment which were built into the blueprint of humanity, and which have been

Introduction

successively discovered and forgotten throughout the ages of mankind.

You do not have to sell your soul to the devil, or do anything unholy or dangerous. Neither do you have to become a saint and give up anything that makes life worth living for you.

I will show you how to employ the seas of energy which had been invisible and undetected until recent years, when researchers rediscovered these radiations and even photographed them.

Long before modern science uncovered these energies, however, a few fortunate people were using them to achieve their every desire.

Some were dedicated scientists who slowly solved the hidden mysteries and used them to grow in stature, wealth, and happiness. Others, almost by accident, had the secret and used it without realizing it; we say they are the types who are born with silver spoons in their mouths.

Now it's your turn.

YOU CAN USE THESE SECRET ENERGIES FOR ANYTHING YOU DESIRE

You may have read other books of mine. Each one was another attempt to show how you can reach harmony with the universe and be happy by connecting yourself with cosmic energies. And, like any other genuine researcher, I've never stopped refining the methods.

I've dropped some concepts which, although they were useful and valuable in their time, have since been seen to be unnecessarily clumsy or

Introduction

complicated. Over the years, I've been seeking—and finding—simpler and more logical methods to reach happiness and contentment.

On the way I researched other disciplines, some of which have been in existence for eons, and others of which came on the scene in recent years, as other researchers traveled their own paths of investigation.

All of this led me to *Acupineology*, a long word which rhymes with "Jack, you find dollar fee." It's a word combined of "Acu," meaning a point, as in *acupuncture*; "pine," the first four letters of *pineal*, the mystic gland in your brain which is keyed to psychic powers; and "ology," a science or branch of learning.

You are reading the first handbook of Acupineology, showing you how to identify psychic points and scientifically tune yourself to the natural power which I have named *Iso-Bionic Energy.*

This is an invisible energy, like most other forms of energy. No matter where you are, you're always being positively bombarded with energy.

Some of it you use to cook food, to light your room, to get a suntan, to hear music, to watch the late-late show. But there are many other energies, and astrologers have had a handle on them for centuries.

What's happening today is that the energies which astrologers have been saying are part and parcel of our lives are being detected by scientific means.

Sober researchers now confirm that different forms of energy previously known only to mystics are

Introduction

pouring down on us from the rest of the universe, and that they also pulse and shimmer around every living thing.

These are the energies of creation, the powers that keep this solar system operating better than the smoothest running machine ever made by the hand of man.

They may have been a secret, but now they're yielding up their mysteries rapidly. And a few people are already using these energies to shape their lives into incredible success patterns.

That's precisely what this book is all about. Simply, easily, and quickly, you can reach out for these invisible energies.

You will instantly become as serene and peaceful as the moon, swinging faultlessly around the earth. You will absorb your share of the total harmony of the universe, and your life will become totally harmonious in sympathy.

Anything you desire will be yours to command. Decide on your need, connect with the energies with simple gestures, words, and postures, and you've literally got it. Fate swings into action on your behalf, and your fondest dreams become reality.

PAIN, PENURY, AND FRUSTRATION BANISHED FOREVER

Pain is nature's signal that something is wrong with you. The natural harmony of your body has been upset, something is uncomfortable, you're suffering from unease, or (if you like) *dis*ease. Put the disharmony right and the pain goes away.

Introduction

That's an easily understood example of what happens when you're out of step with universal energy fields. Now, come one step further: instead of physical pain, consider mental pain.

Once again, that's a type of pain which will go away if conditions are corrected.

Mental pain can come from many sources. Lack of money, for example, brings all manner of anguish, worry, and harassment. Lack of progress can produce frustration, anger, sorrow, envy, and other destructive emotions. And they *hurt*. They can hurt so much in your mind that the mental agony is reflected in your body, and you develop physical symptoms of a condition which started in your mind.

Worried people develop very real ulcers. Some researchers see a connection between what's going on in the patient's mind and the development of cancer. In fact, with many diseases that seem to be brought on or aggravated by the state of the mind of the sufferer, some doctors are beginning to theorize that almost all afflictions may have their origin in the mind of the patient.

So you can easily understand that your reactions to external conditions can bring on pain, and we've already seen that pain is a sign that the sufferer is not using universal energies as they should be used.

The joyful conclusion I've reached after years of looking at this problem is that attaining harmony with universal energy is no big deal. It's easy and quick.

Literally with a flick of your fingers, you can make energy flow in the right direction so that pain

Introduction

goes away. And once the pain goes, your life becomes calmer, more progressive, and more harmonious, all the way up the scale to euphoric happiness and delight.

Say farewell to pain, penury, and frustration. Welcome peace, fulfillment, and health as you use the science of Acupineology.

CHAOS TRANSFORMED TO HARMONY IN A FEW MINUTES A DAY

Life can be hard in these uncertain, troubled times. I'm about to show you how to change all that. The times may remain troubled, but you'll find yourself untouched by them, free as the air, and if enough of my readers turn their lives around and find the proffered peace and harmony, we may even see the troubles of the world diminishing.

The principals of one well-known mind discipline, preached all over the world, always try to get ten percent of the population of a city or particular area to practice their special type of meditation. That brings its own kind of cosmic harmony. Time after time, statistics have shown that if one person in every ten starts these particular techniques, a kind of psychic groundswell begins, and even people who are not involved in the program start getting benefits.

Crime rates drop. Employment figures pick up. Strikes, lockouts, and work stoppages decrease. Admissions to hospitals diminish. Less people are injured in road and industrial accidents. The suicide graph dips. Business bankruptcies lessen.

Introduction

But, before you can spread such miracles around your local community, your first task is to get yourself on the path to ultimate delight and satisfaction.

I know you must be troubled in some way. Otherwise, you would not need this book. Some part of your life is unsatisfactory. Together, step by step, we're going to change all that, and when you reach the pinnacle of perfection you're setting out for at this moment, you'll have the ultimate pleasure of knowing you did it all for yourself.

Will this program of self-help take up all of your spare time, or keep you from enjoying life? It will not. Right from the start, you will enjoy life *more*, and as you become more harmonious, you'll become more efficient at everyday tasks. You'll have more leisure to enjoy, not less.

All you need to do is allocate about ten minutes a day to carrying out the techniques I describe. These few minutes represent your daily iso-bionic workout. Some of the other exciting life-changing techniques may take a little longer to carry out, but you can schedule those as and when you wish. Only the basic ten minute exercise is a daily essential.

The results may astound you. Your present discomfort may waft away, never to return.

**ISO-BIONIC ENERGY IS REAL
AND SCIENCE IS INTERESTED**

A few words of reassurance here for the doubtful, skeptical, or even fearful. Iso-bionic energy is real. It's being made visible with the right equipment. It is being used daily in North America

Introduction

by recognized healing practitioners who have brought an ancient technique to the West from the Far East.

I mention this because, although some of the things you're going to learn have been part of palmistry, numerology, and astrology from way back when, the energy fields you'll be working with are part of scientific fact today. We are not trespassing into any areas which might offend anyone's religious sensibilities.

I'm well aware that many people have been taught that involvement with "psychic" matters is "the work of the devil." I personally differ from that view. I agree that such things as black magic exist, and that is indeed satanic and anti-religious. I would not touch it with a ten-foot pole. I also believe that there's such a thing as white magic, the power to heal the sick, to bring harmony out of chaos, to banish pain, and to bring about a personal state of joy which is everyone's birthright.

But, although the changes we're going to see you work for yourself may seem magical, I want you to understand that we're working in a field of science which is daily gaining support from hard-headed practical scientists and laboratory personnel.

Kirlian Photography

You may have already heard of Kirlian photography. By using high frequency electrical impulses, color photographs can be taken of the brilliant energy fields which surround all living things.

For centuries, people working in the field of the occult have been attesting that human beings, ani-

Introduction

mals, and plants have colored energy fields, known as auras, around them. By "reading" the aura, a good psychic can estimate the health or sickness of a person.

Kirlian photography now enables us to actually fix those auras on photographic film.

I will not be asking you to spend good money on the equipment necessary to photograph your surrounding energy fields, but I thought you should know that the fields do exist and are being scientifically studied.

My part in the process will be to hand you valid methods of changing your energy fields. As they change for the better, so will your life!

Acupuncture

The Chinese method of healing which stimulates important points on the body with needles is known as acupuncture. The technique changes the energy flows around the body, regulating them to bring about the banishment of diseased conditions.

Acupuncture is a highly specialized science which takes years of training and work. Again, I will not expect you to take a long and expensive course in that science of healing. But I will be showing you points on your body which will stimulate your isobionic energies and get the vitality flowing in the right directions. As we have seen, once your invisible energies are flowing correctly, your very existence will take on new meaning, new success, and new contentment.

Introduction

Biofeedback

You may also have heard of biofeedback. You may even have tried this interesting science, where you learn to change your brainwaves by mental and physical discipline.

Generally speaking, when a person is at rest, unstressed and calm, a particular type of electrical activity appears in the brain.

The other side of that coin is that if you can learn to deliberately turn on that type of electrical activity, then your body and mind automatically become relaxed and peaceful, and the natural energies of the body have a maximum chance of clearing up any dis-ease which exists.

Without having to buy any electronic gizmos to detect the alpha waves, which is a feature of biofeedback, this book will show you how to simply turn on this harmony-producing flow of mental energy. The results of even a small surge of such activity can be amazing, as you'll soon find out.

ACUPINEOLOGY NEEDS NO APPARATUS

Kirlian photography, acupuncture, and biofeedback are only three examples of the many ways natural energy is being used to bring better conditions to people. You should know when you're applying the simple methods of Acupineology that you're working in line with scientific research which is going on right now.

Unlike many other methods, Acupineology requires no expensive equipment, nor do you need to have a college education to understand and use it

Introduction

for your total benefit. On the contrary, if you can read these words, that's all the education you need to become an expert with this new science of natural energy utilization.

GESTURES, CARESSES, SIMPLE MASSAGE, AND WORDS ARE ALL YOU NEED

You may wonder how we are going to apply this science to your life. I've assured you that you do not have to buy any expensive gadgets, and neither do you have to go to college and learn a whole new set of subjects, taking years of your time.

To apply Acupineology, you already have everything you need: your mind and your body, and this book.

Using your hands and fingers in simple gestures, caresses, and massage, all of which I'll explain and reveal point by point, you're going to find out just how sweet life can be for you.

We will also add some verbal sounds to the gestures, to strengthen the flows of iso-bionic energy.

These sounds will also be carefully explained, and you do not have to worry if your command of language is not as clear and precise as that of your local radio announcer!

The way you make the sounds is specifically defined by your throat, air cavities, mouth, teeth (or lack of them!), and tongue. In fact, no one else can make your Acupineology sounds for you. The way you make them is geared to you alone, uniquely and definitely. And it's you who are seeking the benefits,

Introduction

so the whole process is sharply focused on you and your personal iso-bionic energy.

Along with that focus and the new flows of energy come your personal miracles, inevitably, automatically, and joyfully.

RIDE THE CREST OF THE WAVE WITH ACUPINEOLOGY

If I said that the heights you can reach with Acupineology are limited only by your imagination, I'd be wrong. Time after time I hear of people who have found success after using iso-bionic energy, and their response has been: "It's even *better* than I could have imagined."

At this point in time you may have a mental picture of how you wish your life could be. I wonder if you're aiming too low. Life has perhaps taught you what some cynics call a "truth." They say, "Blessed are they who expect nothing, for they shall not be disappointed."

That's a cruel and self-diminishing thought. You deserve better than you have now, but although you may aspire to better things, experience has probably drilled home the message that you should not expect too much. That way, you're not so hurtfully disillusioned when your fondest dreams crumble into ashes.

If that's your outlook, Acupineology is for you. By all means, set up a self-improvement program and let iso-bionic energy carry you toward it. I know one thing for sure: if you'll give it ten minutes a day, Acupineology will go one better than your most

Introduction

glittering hope, and lift you into realms of contentment you hardly dared to consider.

Your hopeful wish for a little more peace, a roof over your head, a few spare dollars in the bank, and a harmonious, undemanding partner can be parlayed by Acupineology into a sparkling stream of good fortune and life achievement that puts your present dreams in the shade.

Another certainty is that regular application of Acupineology will change your life for the better. Take the time to write down where and how you wish to be in one year's time. Then write down where you honestly *think* you'll be this time next year, if things go on along the same old path. Write down the date and tuck the paper into the back of this book.

Then, apply Acupineology, and read that set of notes later on. You'll fully understand how iso-bionic energy takes you along joyful paths you had never even considered.

You're about to find the perfect wave, to ride blissfully into an expanding, stimulating future where destiny obeys your every whim. Where you're going to travel, the sky is not the limit—it's only the beginning of rapture and delight and the achievement of happiness which so many pursue and so few attain.

Introduction

Table of Contents

VcToria's Foreword 1

INTRODUCTION: HOW THIS BOOK CAN BRING YOU HAPPINESS, HEALTH, FREEDOM, AND MATERIAL SUCCESS 2

   YOU CAN USE THESE SECRET ENERGIES FOR ANYTHING YOU DESIRE 3

   PAIN, PENURY, AND FRUSTRATION BANISHED FOREVER 5

   CHAOS TRANSFORMED TO HARMONY IN A FEW MINUTES A DAY 7

   ISO-BIONIC ENERGY IS REAL AND SCIENCE IS INTERESTED 8

      Kirlian Photography 9

      Acupuncture 10

      Biofeedback 11

   ACUPINEOLOGY NEEDS NO APPARATUS 11

   GESTURES, CARESSES, SIMPLE MASSAGE, AND WORDS ARE ALL YOU NEED 12

   RIDE THE CREST OF THE WAVE WITH ACUPINEOLOGY 13

ACU-KEY 1: ALL YOUR TROUBLES VANISH WHEN YOU BALANCE YOUR ISO-BIONIC ENERGIES 25

   ISO-BIONIC ENERGY PERVADES YOUR ENTIRE WORLD 27

   WHAT THE VARIOUS CURRENTS AND ENERGY FIELDS CAN DO FOR YOU 28

Contents

    Your psinic field 29

    Your pectoral field 29

    Your umbilical field... 29

WHICH OF YOUR FIELDS NEEDS STIMULATING? .. 30

GESTURES BRING YOUR ENERGY FIELDS UP TO MAXIMUM STRENGTH... 32

    Your umbilical gesture 33

    Your pectoral gesture 33

    Your psinic gesture.. 34

    Performing more than one gesture 34

    An outdoor method of charging all three fields...... 35

HOW TO CREATE YOUR PSINIC VIBRATION 36

HOW TO CREATE YOUR PECTORAL SWELL........... 38

HOW TO CREATE YOUR UMBILICAL RESONANCE . 39

DECIDE ON YOUR DESIRE AND REACH OUT FOR IT 40

ACU-KEY 2: USING YOUR DIGITAL ACTIVATORS AUTOMATICALLY OPENS THE ROAD TO YOUR PERSONAL SHANGRI-LA 43

    ISO-BIONIC ENERGY AT THREE LEVELS OF BEING 46

    HOW TO MAKE YOUR ISO-BIONIC PLANETARY CONNECTIONS 46

        Figure 1: Planetary Names on the Human Hand ... 48

    NATURAL FOUNTAINS OF WEALTH, FREEDOM, AND HEALTH FOR YOU 49

    SENSITIZING PROCESS TO ASSIST YOUR ISO-BIONIC ENERGY FLOW 52

Contents

HANDS, FINGERS, AND OTHER BODILY CONTACT FOR STARTLING PERSONAL MIRACLES.................. 54

    Figure 2. Planetary Correspondences.................... 56

WHAT HAPPENS WHEN YOU MAKE A PLANETARY CONTACT 57

ACU-KEY 3: THE EXPANSIVE TOUCH OF JUPITER BRINGS YOU UNLIMITED CASH AND POSSESSIONS 61

    POWER UNLIMITED FROM THE JUPITER GESTURE 64

    ATTRACTING RICH PARTNERS WITH THE JUPITER CONNECTION 66

    JUPITER MASSAGE MAKES SURE YOU'RE THE ONE WHO WINS 68

    THE JUPITER CONNECTION PERFORMANCE HAS BEEN FOLLOWED BY HEALING 70

    JUPITER CONNECTIONS SHOW YOU EXACTLY HOW TO WIN AT NUMBERS, LOTTERIES, OR SWEEPSTAKES 75

    HOW TO PRESERVE YOUR NEW-FOUND WEALTH.. 81

ACU-KEY 4: ACHIEVE TRUE PEACE, FREEDOM, AND LOVE WITH THE AMAZING POLLEX TECHNIQUES .. 83

    REACTIONS AND EMOTIONS................................ 85

    BREAK ALL RESTRICTIONS WITH POLLEX-INSPIRED WILLPOWER 86

    POLLEX CONTACT SHIELDS NEGATIVITY 87

        Aggravating husband.. 89

        Aggravating wife... 89

        Intimidating official 89

        Stage fright 90

Contents

    Annoying children 90

    Afraid to speak out 90

    Overstayed welcome 90

USE SEVERAL MOUNTS IF NECESSARY 90

POLLEX MASSAGE POINTS BRING SURGING NATURAL ENERGY 92

    Umbilical massage point 93

    Lower back massage points 94

    Shoulder pollex massage 94

POLLEX PRESSURE POINT HOLDS PAIN AT BAY 95

BANISH FEARS AND PHOBIAS WITH THIS POLLEX CONTACT 97

ALL NEGATIVE CONDITIONS DISSOLVE WHEN YOU USE POLLEX CONTACTS 98

ACU-KEY 5: MOON TECHNIQUES QUICKLY BRING VAST PROFITS 99

CONFUSED? MOON MASSAGE MAKES EVERYTHING CLEAR 102

    You can control destiny with Moon massage 102

    Moon massage technique 103

MAKE THE MOON CONTACT AND BECOME A SUPER-SNOOPER 105

    Moon contact technique 105

    Know your brain type 106

    Continued Moon contact technique 108

    You have opened up a hot line 108

Contents

MOON CONNECTIONS LOCATE HIDDEN TREASURE 109
DETECT PRIVATE SECRETS WITH MOON CONTACT 113
MOON TECHNIQUES ARE IRRESISTIBLE UNLESS YOU KNOW THIS SECRET 115

ACU-KEY 6: SPECIALIZED MOON CONCEPTS FOR TAKING PROFITABLE PSYCHIC JOURNEYS 119

ASTRAL TRAVEL CUTS THE SURLY BONDS OF EARTH 121
GIANT STEPS TOWARD YOUR GOALS WITH THE ASTRAL VISITATION 123
USE AKASHIC AWARENESS TO TALK TO MYSTIC BEINGS 127
HAVE YOU LIVED BEFORE? 129
   Discover your reincarnation path 129
   Travel to other times and places 130
   Another life? 132
PREVIOUS INCARNATION KNOWLEDGE CAN MEAN MONEY IN THE BANK 133
DREAM GUIDING AND MIND TOUCHING: TWIN HIGHROADS TO THE TOP 134
   Dream guiding 135
   Mind touching 136
SAFETY FROM MIND INTRUSION WITH THIS MOON DEFENSE 139

ACU-KEY 7: ADDITIONAL SHATTERING STRENGTH FROM ALPHA-NUMERIC TONES 141

Contents

AS ABOVE, SO BELOW 143

THE RIGHT SOUND REELS IN YOUR WISH 144

THE ALPHA-TONES FOR YOUR PSINIC VIBRATION 145

THE BETA-TONES FOR YOUR PECTORAL SWELL .. 146

THE SIGMA-TONES FOR YOUR UMBILICAL
RESONANCE 147

NOW ADD THE MAGIC OF NUMEROLOGY 148

    Year vibration number 148

    Month vibration number 149

    Day vibration number 149

THE RIGHT TONE FOR THE RIGHT DAY 150

    Alpha-tone numbers 150

    Beta-tone numbers 151

    Sigma-tone numbers 152

INCREDIBLE ENERGY IS YOURS TO COMMAND ... 152

ACU-KEY 8: HELP YOURSELF TO MIRACLES BY USING SURPLUS ENERGY FROM OTHER PEOPLE .. 153

ISO-BIONIC ENERGY EBBS AND FLOWS 155

YOUR ISO-BIONIC TIDEWAY 156

WHEN TO USE YOUR TIDEWAY GESTURE 158

ADD THESE TECHNIQUES TO YOUR TIDEWAY
GESTURE FOR EVEN MORE EXTRAORDINARY
RESULTS 160

HOW TO DRAW ISO-BIONIC ENERGY FROM A SOCIAL
HANDSHAKE 162

WHAT COMES NEXT? 163

Contents

YOUR ACUPINEOLOGY PROGRAM BRINGS RICHES AT ALL LEVELS OF BEING 165

SOLAR SYSTEMIC NODES MAKE YOU THE BIG WINNER 167

 Astrology lore 168

 Your birthday 169

 Eight solar systemic nodes 170

TURN THE PAGE TO START YOUR MIRACLE-WORKING 172

ACU-KEY 9: YOUR CUSTOM-CRAFTED PROGRAM OF TOWERING SUCCESS 173

NOTE YOUR SOLAR SYSTEMIC NODE PERIODS ... 175

VIBRATION NUMBER OF THE DAY 176

TONES FOR THE DAY 177

YOUR DAILY ACUPINEOLOGY WORKOUT 178

TURNING YOUR LIFE AROUND 178

OPPORTUNITIES FOR ISO-BIONIC ENERGY BOOSTS 179

SPECIFIC MIRACLES 179

 Physical health (pectoral field) 180

 Mental harmony (psinic field) 180

 Spiritual growth (umbilical field) 181

 Emotional harmony (psinic field) 181

 Material expansion (pectoral field) 182

THE ULTIMATE SECRET 182

AN ACUPINEOLOGY NOTEBOOK 183

Contents

Nick W.'s Notebook 184
ACUPINEOLOGY USES ONLY HOLY, CREATIVE ENERGY 185
BE GENEROUS WITH YOUR NEW-FOUND POWERS 186
TRANSFORMING DISCOMFORT TO DELIGHT IS ACUPINEOLOGY'S PRIME OBJECTIVE 188
PERFECTION BECKONS, SO SAVOR IT TO THE FULLEST 189

All Your Troubles Vanish When You Balance Your Iso-Bionic Energies

If you read the introduction to this book, you already know some of its basic aims. But, if you're one of those people who dives into the "meat" of a book and you started reading on this page, I can outline my theme in a few words.

ISO-BIONIC ENERGY PERVADES YOUR ENTIRE WORLD

Just as a mighty hydroelectric plant takes the energy of water and transforms it into power to turn the wheels of industry, so does your body transform the energy in food into power to keep your "wheels" turning. That energy enables you to move around, to carry weights, to breathe, to pump blood through your veins and arteries, to talk, to hear, to see, and to think.

Some of your natural energy is used physically by your muscles, while other portions of your generated energy literally keep your body and soul together.

In the process of working, your body and mind radiate an energy field, which was identified earlier as your *aura*. As long as your life energy is flowing along smoothly, you stay healthy, well, and contented.

All Your Troubles Vanish

With the permission of a dedicated metaphysical researcher, Evelyn Hudson, whose insightful work helped me to refine and perfect this book, I have named the unseen natural power *iso-bionic energy*. You will be employing this energy to transform your existence into perfect shape.

Only under special conditions can you see, feel, or hear your iso-bionic energy, but its effects are very apparent in other ways. For example, when you meet a stranger and instantly love or hate him without rhyme or reason, that's a signal that your individual iso-bionic energies are harmonizing or conflicting.

Your iso-bionic energy fields spread out around your body and interact with everything and everyone who affects your life, whether he be a partner in your own office or some bureaucrat far away, drafting new tax laws which can affect your standard of living.

If your iso-bionic energies are flowing freely and clearly, in harmony with the universe, you will be lucky, happy, and fulfilled. If your energy fields are not in tune with exterior conditions, you will meet with frustration, opposition, sadness, and loss.

Simply stated, the goal of this book is to show you exactly how to keep your iso-bionic energies working *for* you instead of *against* you.

WHAT THE VARIOUS CURRENTS AND ENERGY FIELDS CAN DO FOR YOU

You're going to learn how to use iso-bionic energy to help you join in with the favored people of this world.

All Your Troubles Vanish

We shall be looking at the various energy flows in and around you, and discovering exactly what to do with them to bring you what you need.

Broadly speaking, you have three energy fields flowing through your body, each connected with various areas of your life. Each field is made up of currents or *lines of force*; just as a piece of cloth is woven from separate strands of cotton. The lines of force we shall be using flow from and to important, easily located points on your hands and fingers.

Your psinic field

Your *psinic* (pronounced "sigh-nick") *field* flows back and forth between your hands and your face. Its lines of force are associated with all mental processes and are very powerfully concentrated at a point in the center of your forehead about an inch above your eyebrows. That point is your *psinic focus.*

Your pectoral field

Your *pectoral* (pronounced "peck-troll") *field* forms a web of energy between your chest and your hands and is connected with material things that you can see, touch, smell, taste, or hear. A point midway between your nipples is your *pectoral focus,* where the lines of force converge into a forceful beam of power.

Your umbilical field

Your umbilical (pronounced "um-billy-cool") field flows from the area around your navel to and from your hands. It is associated with abstract concepts, such as spiritual growth, and all other aspects of life which are not the province of the other two fields. Your navel is your umbilical focus, where the lines of force unite into an invisible, potent stream.

WHICH OF YOUR FIELDS NEEDS STIMULATING?

A Nobel Prize-winning scientist once remarked, "The laws of nature are so simple, we have to rise above the complexity of scientific thought to see them." In other words, we often try too hard to explain or understand something, and we end up confused, when what we're looking at is basically simple and straightforward.

Keep that thought in mind when you're using the iso-bionic energy fields. As natural energy, they *are* simple, yet they defy explanation. Your simple task is to use the energies, and you can leave the explanations to someone who has more time, interest, and energy. I agree that the reasons behind the miraculous powers of iso-bionic energy should be researched, but initially it's far more satisfying for you to concentrate on using it to make yourself happy.

The simple fact of iso-bionic energy is that once you smooth it out, it flows. Your life, mind, body, and soul become content, healthy, dynamic, and fulfilled.

When you decide which area of your life needs changing for the better, move in to stimulate the energy fields, make the sounds, gestures, and movements described step-by-step in later chapters, and your life will automatically take a gigantic turn for the better.

All Your Troubles Vanish

For example, you may decide you need a new car. That's a material thing that you can see and touch. Your pectoral field is in that domain, and techniques associated with that field will ensure that a car is placed among your future possessions, sometimes by a succession of amazing coincidences which finally convince you of the incredible powers of iso-bionic energy.

Alternatively, you may wish to bring a lover to your side. That involves emotion, which goes on chiefly at mental levels. You should then involve yourself with psinic field techniques, and destiny will unerringly bring you a partner who is everything you've ever fantasized, and then some!

Perhaps you're suffering from something very intangible, such as the "divine discontent" that poet Charles Kingsley describes so graphically in his works. More simply, maybe you're unable to put your finger on what's wrong with your life. That's a clear case for using your umbilical field to align destiny with whatever is needed to allow you to feel gloriously free and happy.

I would not advise you to be too concerned about which field to use at any one time. All three are composed of the same kind of energy, and they will all work for you. If you choose to use your pectoral field to bring you a lover because you decide that a lover would be something you can see and touch rather than a true emotional involvement, no harm is done. Maybe you'll need to pour on the power a bit longer or stronger to attain your desired result, but in the end it will not be critically important.

All Your Troubles Vanish

It would be better for you to go ahead and use any one of the fields, rather than spend days debating about exactly which field would be best. In fact, later on, when you get into the swing of this startling process, you'll be amazed at how simply and easily you can tune in unconsciously to any field and continue to get precisely what you need.

Each field does have its special purpose, but they will all take over and deal with other areas if necessary.

GESTURES BRING YOUR ENERGY FIELDS UP TO MAXIMUM STRENGTH

All three of the energy fields described earlier flow through your hands, and some psychics, especially those who are into yoga, say they can clearly see the lines of force radiating from the human hand.

By simple placement of your fingers and palms, you can charge up your energy fields at any time, so that when they are called on, they will be fully charged and raring to go to work on your personal miracles.

Fortunately, all three of these gestures are "natural" ones. You can perform them at any time, without the rest of the world even noticing anything unusual. At any spare moment of the day or night, when you have nothing else to do for a couple of minutes or so, you can use these energy-building gestures. The results, when you call on your iso-bionic energy, will be that much more effective.

Your umbilical gesture

To charge your umbilical field, clasp your hands together and lay your palms flat across your navel. This gesture is performed in precisely the same way as a person who has had a good meal sits back and puts his hands on his stomach, saying, "That was good!"

Try the gesture once and you'll understand what I'm telling you. Of course, you do not have to say, "That was good." You say nothing at all.

As you put your hands in position, close your eyes, relax your muscles, and breathe deeply five times. Return your breathing to its regular tempo and depth, keeping your eyes closed. Two minutes is long enough to hold the gesture. A longer time will not add much to the total power in your umbilical field, but if you wish to continue to hold the gesture, by all means do so. However, do *not* continue to breathe deeply—you'll hyperventilate, taking on more oxygen than your body can easily handle, and you will make yourself dizzy. As a rule, should you find your head spinning even slightly while you're doing any of these gestures, stop the deep breathing at once and allow everything to swing back to normal.

Your pectoral gesture

The technique for charging your pectoral field is very similar to the foregoing gesture. The clasped fingers are identical, except that they are held higher up on your body, across and in contact with your chest, covering your pectoral focus.

You can move directly from the umbilical gesture to the pectoral gesture merely by sliding your clasped hands about eight inches up your chest until they come to rest with the heels of your palms covering your nipples.

Hold this position and take five deep breaths, with your eyes closed and your muscles as relaxed as possible. Hold the gesture for two minutes.

Your psinic gesture

Your psinic field is charged with your hands held in a different position. Bring your open hands up on either side of your head and gently place your thumbs against your cheeks, just in front of your ear. Your fingers should be pointing up and forward.

Fold your hands around until your little fingers touch each other and also touch your forehead about an inch above your eyebrows.

Spread the rest of your fingers comfortably and allow them to touch your head. Rest your elbows on a table or the arms of your chair if that can be arranged without difficulty.

Take five deep breaths after closing your eyes and allowing your body to relax. Hold the gesture for about two minutes.

Performing more than one gesture

If you so desire, you can charge up more than one field at a time as you perform these gestures. In such a case, you are required to take five deep breaths *once only*, whether you're charging up two of your fields or all three of them.

What you're wearing is unimportant. Iso-bionic energy penetrates clothing, so there's no need to strip to the waist to perform these gestures.

All Your Troubles Vanish

If you do them each once, in the order described, you'll realize that they're a perfectly natural sequence of positions which people often adopt, so you can safely charge up your fields in public, without anyone else being the wiser.

Even if someone notices you performing the gestures, the most they're likely to think of the psinic gesture is that you're thinking deeply on some weighty subject, or that maybe you're checking to see if your bill was added up correctly!

An outdoor method of charging all three fields

This routine is tremendously powerful and brings incredible vitality to your energy fields. It is best performed when no one else is around, because it can look a little strange to the uninitiated.

It must also be performed in the open air. You need to find a convenient tree, preferably an evergreen. If it has needles, like a pine tree, so much the better. A Christmas tree in a pot is not suitable; your tree needs to be growing from the natural earth.

The final condition to seek is that at least one branch of the tree must be no more than four feet or so from the ground, within your reach as you stand in front of it.

Walk up to the tree with your arms spread wide, hands open and palms turned forward, as you would greet a long-lost friend after a separation. Arrange your position so that both hands are gently touching the foliage.

Turn your face upward, close your eyes, and as you feel the leaves or needles brushing your palms,

All Your Troubles Vanish

take five deep breaths. Hold that position for about a minute, or slightly longer if you wish.

Be careful now! You've picked up a very powerful charge of energy from the tree, and it can literally set you back on your heels. First, move your head *gently and slowly* forward until, when you open your eyes, you're looking straight ahead, on a level.

Then, *and only then*, open your eyes. Check for a moment to see that you have your balance and that you are not too dizzy to step away. If your head is spinning, stay where you are until everything stops going around. If necessary, hold onto the tree for support.

When your world is steady, step away from the tree, lower your hands, turn to your *right*, and walk away.

You can, if you wish, thank the tree for giving you a share of its iso-bionic energy, but if you feel that's a dumb thing to do, forget about it.

VcToria Comments: *I would thank the tree. I do not find that a dumb thing to do at all. Trees supply our oxygen and energy.*

HOW TO CREATE YOUR PSINIC VIBRATION

This whole universe is made up of vibrations of various amplitudes and speeds, and your iso-bionic energy is no exception. You can stimulate and direct it to carry out your will by the use of simple vocal sounds.

You do not have to be a trained singer to do this simple energy reinforcement. If you can talk, you can create a *psinic vibration.*

All Your Troubles Vanish

Take a deep breath. Say "Eeeeeeeeee!" and keep the sound going, turning it into a kind of high, singing tone. Do not make it too high or screechy. You do not need to squeak so that your throat aches.

Your psinic vibration is very quiet. Once you've got the "E" sound going, close your lips and keep the sound humming through your nose. Carry on with it until you need to take another breath.

Please do not strain. Holding the vibration until your lungs are bursting for air is not the idea. Just hold the vibration for a maximum of 20 seconds after you close your lips. Ten seconds is long enough, and even five will do, if you're short of wind.

Repeat the sound two more times, and you've done one complete psinic vibration.

When you get the hang of it, you'll actually feel it vibrating inside your head, in the sinus cavities behind your nose.

If your nose is blocked for any reason, such as a head cold, keep your lips slightly apart and let the sound carry from your mouth.

Some people find that if they hold their teeth gently together a good, resonating psinic vibration also vibrates their teeth.

Experiment with a higher or lower note until, when you cover your ears with your hands, the sound fills your whole head. Note that putting your hands over your ears is not part of the psinic vibration; it's merely a test to carry out when you're first getting accustomed to making the vibration effective.

It's possible that you may not have use of your vocal cords, and cannot utter the necessary sound. In your case, merely *thinking* the sound will be equally effective. But, if you have a voice, use it for this powerful energy-peaking exercise.

HOW TO CREATE YOUR PECTORAL SWELL

The *pectoral swell* is somewhat similar to your psinic vibration, except that you use a different letter sound, a lower tone, and you keep your lips open while you're creating the swell.

Take a deep breath. Now "sing" the letter "A," sounding it as a tone, just as you did with the psinic vibration. This time, however, keep your lips parted. You should be intoning "A," not "Ah." If you're in any doubt about this, start by saying the letter "K," which makes the right kind of "A" sound.

It does not matter in the slightest if you're unable to "carry a tune in a bucket." All that is required is your best effort at holding the "A" tone, and if your vocal cords are not working, you may "think" the sound, as I suggested for the psinic vibration.

The sound of your pectoral swell is lower than the psinic vibration. It is not a *basso profundo* groan, however, just a mid-range tone which you hold quietly until you need to breathe again. Repeat this two more times, and that completes your pectoral swell.

To check on whether the swell is coming from the right part of your body, run your fingers up the center of your chest from the lower edge of your rib cage toward your throat.

About four inches below your collarbone, you should be able to feel the vibration of your pectoral swell. If you feel nothing, try putting your fingers under your clothes, in contact with your bare flesh.

If you still fail to detect any vibrations under your fingers, try lowering the tone a bit. Experiment a little and eventually you'll find it. You'll distinctly feel vibrations in the bones and flesh of your upper chest. Feeling for the swell with your fingers is merely an initial test and does not form part of your regular production of the pectoral swell.

I have said that the pectoral swell can be done quietly, and that's true. But if you're alone where no one can overhear you, by all means, let yourself go with this one. But, remember, no straining. If your throat aches or your voice turns hoarse after you've done a pectoral swell completely, go easier on yourself—you're trying too hard.

HOW TO CREATE YOUR UMBILICAL RESONANCE

Your *umbilical resonance* may take a little practice, but if you follow these simple instructions, it will come naturally.

Take a deep breath. Now, *whisper* the letter "M," making it a long, drawn out exhalation of breath, and not completing the closed-lips "Mmm" part of the letter until you're ready to stop and take another breath. You'll probably be able to stretch this out for as long as five seconds.

Do it again, but this time relax your throat and turn the whisper into the lowest tone you can manage, a deep down tone—but do not turn it into a throat-tearing croak. Do not strain, just relax, and let your voice make the deepest note you can reach comfortably. As you persist, you'll be able to produce quite a respectable breathy rumble, coming from deep down inside you.

A complete umbilical resonance consists of taking a deep breath, saying—or rumbling!—the long "M," and then repeating it twice more.

Practice at your leisure. I'll be telling you when and how to use this powerful energy-invigorating resonance, plus the psinic vibration and pectoral swell, further along during this course of self-help with iso-bionic energy.

DECIDE ON YOUR DESIRE
AND REACH OUT FOR IT

Let's summarize the simple path you're following toward total life improvement.

You're applying *Acupineology*, a science which deals with iso-bionic energy, an unseen, natural force which affects you and your life state.

You are surrounded by three iso-bionic energy fields, and with the previously described sounds and gestures you can fully charge your psinic, pectoral, and umbilical fields.

Within each field are important lines of force, and the next thing you're going to be shown is how to move your body to intersect different lines of force which are connected with your well-being.

That alignment is going to do amazing things to the way you see and experience the world. Your desires will become sharp and accurate tools to use to carve your future into exactly the shape you wish.

All Your Troubles Vanish

Instead of plodding along day after day, wondering what fresh indignity a malignant fate is going to heap on your bowed head, you will become the true master of your own destiny.

That which you wish for shapes up in the immediate future and then bursts upon you in a delightful shower of luck, happiness, and fulfillment.

So, let's move right along to uncover the next Acu-Key to your total happiness, so that you can decide on your desires, reach for them, and see them come into resplendent actuality.

Using Your Digital Activators Automatically Opens the Road to Your Personal Shangri-La

Our next step closely resembles some of the techniques of the ancient Chinese healing art of acupuncture. But I'm not about to tell you to stick needles in your flesh, the way the Chinese doctors do to bring about their miraculous cures.

Acupuncture, like Acupineology, works with unseen energies. Acupuncturists recognize the force of life that comes into the body at birth, and they call that energy *ch'i.*

They see it flowing in specific and continuous patterns in and around the human body, along channels of energy known as meridians. These meridians can be traced on the surface of the body as lines of force which connect at the acupuncture points where the doctors plant their needles.

Some doctors attest that the acupuncture points can be located by rubbing a sensitive stethoscope over the skin, while others have measured differing skin temperature at these points.

The flow of *ch'i* corresponds to the force of life which the doctors recognize as pervading the entire universe. When a patient is sick, the doctors know that his *ch'i* is not flowing correctly. They calculate which meridian is out of balance, and by implanting needles into points along the meridian, the *ch'i* is balanced and the patient recovers.

ISO-BIONIC ENERGY AT THREE LEVELS OF BEING

Acupineology carries the philosophy and science of acupuncture into your personal life. Not only does the flow of *ch'i* affect your health, but the corresponding flow of iso-bionic energy also affects your physical, mental, and emotional well-being.

By increasing the flow along special lines of force in your iso-bionic energy fields—corresponding to the acupuncture meridians—you can change your entire life, not merely within your mind and body, but in the outside world as well.

Acupuncture uses needles. Acupineology uses your fingers instead, employing them in specific ways to transform them into powerful *digital activators*. By placing your fingers and hands in positions which will be explained to you step by step, you activate the correct flows of iso-bionic energy to bring you what you need.

It is a simple, but incredibly powerful technique. You're merely aligning yourself with natural forces, and the delightful results are automatic.

HOW TO MAKE YOUR ISO-BIONIC PLANETARY CONNECTIONS

People who have studied palmistry, the art of reading the human hand, have named various parts of the hands after the sun, moon, and planets which make up our solar system. Drawing on ancient astrological lore, the fingers and palms have specific areas which connect with spheres of experience that are common to all of us.

Using Your Digital Activators

The sketch of a right hand in Figure 1 shows you the names of the planets and where they are identified on the hand.

Your first finger, the one you usually point with, is called the *Jupiter finger*. Your second finger is your *Saturn finger*, your third finger is your *Sun finger*, and your pinkie is your *Mercury finger*.

Your thumb is allocated to Pluto, while the Moon and the four remaining planets appear on the palm itself.

The fleshy part of your palm below your thumb is known as the *mount of Venus*, while over to the far edge of your palm near your wrist is the *mount of the Moon*.

Further up that same edge of your palm, on the way from the mount of the Moon toward your little finger, is the *mount of Neptune*.

Between the base of your first finger and your thumb is the *mount of Mars*, and the center of your palm is known as the *plain of Uranus*.

Palmistry students will know that a second mount of Mars exists on the palm, but for the purpose of Acupineology, we do not need to identify or use it.

The final thing you need to know is that, as well as naming the fingers after four planets, the fleshy pads on your palm at the base of each finger are also known as mounts, and they carry the same names as the fingers above them.

So, starting at the base of your forefinger and moving across the hand to your pinkie, we find the

Using Your Digital Activators

mounts of Jupiter, Saturn, Sun, and Mercury, in that order.

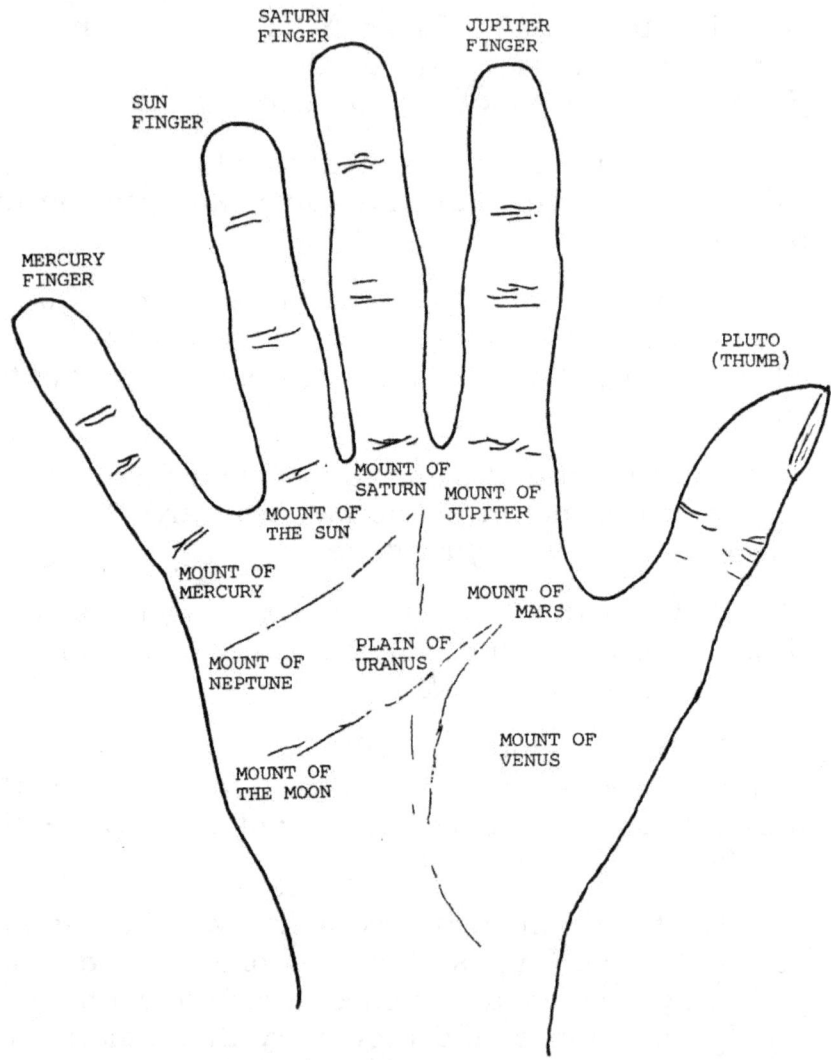

Figure 1: Planetary Names on the Human Hand

Using Your Digital Activators

It would be a good idea to insert a bookmark or a slip of paper into this book at this point, so that you can easily relocate the picture of the palm. The data in Figure 1 is vital to your future success and happiness. Yet, although I've explained the planetary areas of your hand in some detail, you do not have to remember it all. When you are ready to learn the specific techniques, you'll consult Figure 1 and you'll see what you need to do very clearly.

The illustration shows a right hand. Note that the same planets are allocated to the corresponding fingers and areas of the left hand. And there's no need to fuss about whether you're left-handed, right-handed, or even ambidextrous. Iso-bionic energy works in the same way for all human beings.

We know that your iso-bionic energy fields flow along lines of force to and from your hands. You're going to touch appropriate fingers and mounts to other areas, which will cause a cascading stream of iso-bionic energy flow.

That's truly almost all there is to using your digital activators and making your iso-bionic planetary energy flow. The only other area to investigate is exactly where to apply the stimulation.

NATURAL FOUNTAINS OF WEALTH, FREEDOM, AND HEALTH FOR YOU

I'd like to emphasize some points about the incredibly good results to be gained from using Acu-pineology.

If you've never had the luck to experience the good life, or if you've been there once and fate has cast you into the depths of loss and despair, it can

Using Your Digital Activators

be a distinct challenge for you to imagine exactly how you might feel when all the bounty of this miraculous universe pours into your life in a glittering stream of wealth, peace of mind, and freedom from need.

Your doubt may stem from disbelief that spending no more than a few minutes a day on simple exercises could bring luxuries cascading into your life. You've been told, "You can't get something for nothing," and I agree with that old adage. You do need to expend energy to turn it into something real and tangible.

What Acupineology does for you is to use existing energy which is free for the taking.

Let me offer you an example. Let's imagine that you've chopped down a large tree, trimmed the smaller branches, and now you have to move the heavy trunk to a sawmill about a mile away.

There is no way for you to lift that hunk of wood with your bare hands. You might, if you're strong enough, be able to lever the trunk onto rollers and shove and push the timber inch by painful inch cross-country to the mill.

Another solution would be to buy or rent a truck and the necessary lifting machinery, and drive your load to the mill. Again, that would take energy. Besides the energy you'd have to buy in the shape of gasoline for the truck, you'd have to work (using still more energy) to earn the money to rent or buy the transport.

Now, what if you had arranged things so that an existing source of free energy would take your log to the mill, with you having to act only as guide and

Using Your Digital Activators

planner? Imagine that you've planned ahead and chopped down your tree on the bank of a river which happens to flow past the sawmill.

All you have to do now is roll the log into the water and the *natural energy* of the flowing waters will carry your log to where you want it to go. That way, you're getting lots of energy, free for the taking.

This is an example of getting around the "something-for-nothing" idea. Think about it now in terms of Acupineology.

You know that wealth, health, and happiness are out there somewhere. Every day you hear of people who have won millions of dollars in lotteries, found hidden treasure, been given fabulous jobs, discovered their soul mates, and opened up to total happiness in a thousand and one ways.

Yet, so far as you're concerned, you have to struggle on the best you know how, and good fortune is something which happens to other people.

Iso-bionic energy is like that river we used in our examples above. It flows in and around you at all times. Acupineology shows you the simple techniques for letting iso-bionic energy sweep everything you've ever wanted into your life, as naturally and forcefully as the mighty river carries the log to the sawmill.

Will you get something for nothing? Not really. Some kind of energy exchange is required to change anything in your life. That energy exists, and all you have to do is immerse yourself in it and "go with the flow."

Using Your Digital Activators

SENSITIZING PROCESS TO ASSIST YOUR ISO-BIONIC ENERGY FLOW

The effects of the ten minutes a day you spend charging up your iso-bionic energy fields and carrying out the specialized touching of fingers and palms which float you to personal glory, will be enhanced by this sensitizing process.

As your body and limbs become the channels for iso-bionic energy, you will align even more accurately with the flows.

We already know that cloth does not impede the passage of iso-bionic energy. Neither does moisture or dirt, so if you carry out the techniques when your hands are grubby or sweaty, you have no need to worry. The energy will flow just as efficiently.

What *will* help the lines of force to build to their strongest peaks is to sensitize your finger tips in the following manner.

VcToria Comments: *If you have a copy of Figure 1 beside you as you perform these next movements it will be easier.*

Hold your right hand up in front of you, so that you're looking at the palm. Grip your right wrist with your left hand, keeping your left thumb on the back of your wrist and your finger tips on the outside of the wrist.

You're holding the wrist in the region where a doctor takes your pulse. Grip the wrist firmly, close your eyes, and count slowly up to 30.

As you do this, you may be able to feel your heartbeat in your right wrist or left fingers. If so, count about 40 to 50 heartbeats, depending on how

Using Your Digital Activators

fast your pulse is. If you're thrilled and excited at getting involved with this new science, your heart may be galloping along a bit more rapidly than usual.

The idea is to grip the wrist for about 30 seconds, but there's no need to use a stopwatch to time it.

Release your grip and put the tip of your left forefinger (Jupiter finger) in the center of your right palm, on the plain of Uranus.

Keeping your left finger tip in contact with your right palm throughout this routine, run the left Jupiter fingertip lightly across your palm, up to the tip of the right little finger (Mercury finger).

Slide back to the plain of Uranus, and then move your left forefinger up the tip of your right third finger (Sun finger).

Repeat this process for your second (Saturn) finger, and finally run your finger tip in the same way up your right forefinger (Jupiter), and back to the plain of Uranus.

As you do this, you may feel surges or gentle prickles of energy in your right hand and up the fingers.

Repeat the whole process on your left hand, starting by gripping your left wrist for about 30 seconds.

VcToria Comments: *Some people have asked me to explain these movements more clearly. The only wording I found a wee bit confusing was the fact that the Jupiter finger is the one that you need to move all around the hand. Once you have placed it on the* *center area, move it up and down **without** lifting it. The idea is to keep all the energy flowing. Follow Figure 1.*

If you're wearing a watch or bracelet which interferes with your grip, take it off or slide it further up your arm. Rings on your fingers will not interfere with this sensitizing process. Practice this a few times to get the swing of it. It takes far longer to describe than it does to actually carry it out. I will suggest that you perform the sensitizing process before your daily Acupineology workout, which will be described for you later.

HANDS, FINGERS, AND OTHER BODILY CONTACT FOR STARTLING PERSONAL MIRACLES

In later sections of this book we'll be identifying specific contacts which bring your desires within reach. To identify which lines of force you're going to be stimulating, take a look at Figure 2, which tabulates the names of the ten heavenly bodies we located on the palms of your hands. Each planet, satellite, or star listed is connected with various life experiences and objects, which are listed in the right-hand column.

There is no need for you to memorize these, although you'll soon be familiar with several as you use them regularly. Maybe another slip of paper marking the place in this book so you can easily find Figure 2 might be a good idea. You can then turn back easily to this table when you're deciding what particular miracle you'd like to have happen next.

Using Your Digital Activators

VcToria Comments: *If you have bought the book from my website you have been e-mailed an extra Figure 2 so you may print it out.*

The basic idea is that you bring the appropriate area of one hand in contact with the connected area of the other hand.

For example—and later we'll be going into more detail on setting these things in motion—suppose you want to gain prosperity with an invention you've tried marketing without success so far.

Prosperity is the domain of the Jupiter finger, and inventions are connected with the plain of Uranus.

Under the conditions I will describe in later pages, you can bring a sweeping surge of iso-bionic energy cascading through your pectoral field by pressing your right Jupiter finger firmly into your left-hand plain of Uranus.

Here is a second example. Perhaps you wish to attract a lover. The mount of Venus is concerned with both attraction and love. So you would press together your left and right mounts of Venus.

Do you understand the rough idea? Let's suppose you have enemies you wish to eliminate. The Saturn finger rules enemies, among the other items listed. Your thumb (Pluto) is concerned with elimination and destruction. Pressing your right thumb on the left mount of Saturn starts the process going, and your enemies will be vanquished by strokes of bad luck which will leave them reeling.

Using Your Digital Activators

Planet	Correspondence
JUPITER	Luck, prosperity, bureaucrat, lawyer, judge, sports, expansion, generosity, possessions, abundance, protection, finances, justice, optimism.
MARS	Energy, aggression, action, courage, fuel, independence, war, argument.
MERCURY	Children, travel, move, brother, sister, food, occupation, creativity, skill, message, small animals, employees.
MOON	Mother, female partner, public, home, change, emotions.
NEPTUNE	Inspiration, confusion, imagination, acting, plumbing, drains, prophecy, fears, illusions, dreams, hospital, secrets, large animals.
PLUTO	Rebuilding, elimination, legacies, construction, destruction, crime, groups, taxes, insurance, wills.
SATURN	Stability, the elderly, teachers, enemies, boundaries, discipline, persistence, punishment, reputation.
SUN	Male partner, father, males in general, health, employer, boss, entertainment.
URANUS	Surprise, unexpected, rebel, friends, invention, electricity, reform, sudden change.
VENUS	Lover, pleasure, attraction, art, marriage, partner, harmony, love, luxuries.

Figure 2. Planetary Correspondences

Using Your Digital Activators

Maybe you're beginning to see what you're getting into. A cosmic avalanche of good circumstances are poised to envelop you, once you put them into action by stimulating your iso-bionic energy fields.

The foregoing simple examples show you how to make *planetary contacts* by touching your hands together. We'll also discover how you can make planetary body contacts with other people, to help you both reach your goals, or to make sure the other person is instrumental in doing what you require.

WHAT HAPPENS WHEN YOU MAKE A PLANETARY CONTACT

I hope that I am getting my meaning and enthusiasm, through to you. Free, life-changing energy is yours to latch on to. Once you're in the flow, the good things of life will come your way with minimum effort on your part.

If, at present, you're not as fortunate as you would like to be, then you must be suffering from a weakness, blockage, or "kink" in your iso-bionic lines of force. By using the sensitizing process described earlier and then making physical contacts with your hands, you will give the lines of force a clear path to flow along. Your appropriate energy field goes into action, and destiny delivers your needs.

I have been emphasizing that Acupineology is a science, with nothing mystic or occult about it.

I agree that we incorporate some arcane symbols and useful ideas from the ancient arts of astrology and palmistry, because they work. But I

Using Your Digital Activators

would not want you to get the impression that we're working any kind of spooky "magic," or making bargains with angels or devils.

I would be the first to agree that many miracles can be accomplished when one is aligned with the ancient forces that are apparently ruled by mythical beings who have control over our universe and lives. I wrote a book in 1974 based on that very premise[1], and, judging purely by the volume of mail I have received from successful readers, it is a valid method of gaining aid from the etheric planes.

As any genuine researcher should do, I've moved on from that level, simplifying, clarifying, and exploring. *New Avatar Power* is still a part of my life, but I realize now that many people are disturbed or fearful about calling on angels to help them personally. Some suggest, seemingly mistakenly, that calling on angels is the work of the devil—or so I've been solemnly informed.

There are no *mystic beings* to worry about (unless you deliberately set out to meet them as described in Acu-Key 6), no calls on *angelic presences* to disturb you, no arcane Hebrew *words of power* which caused some people to wonder what the words meant.

From the research emerges Acupineology, a scientific, straightforward, and incredibly effective method.

I do not, by the way, deny or dismiss the existence of mystic beings and angels. I'm perfectly sure

---

[1] *The Miracle of New Avatar Power* re-published by his daughter in 2019 by The Alternative Universe.

Using Your Digital Activators

that they're seeing that our universe unfolds as it should. They are probably somewhere closely involved in the miracles which Acupineology produces, for after all, iso-bionic energy is only a name for a natural energy which others call Christ consciousness or God power.

So, rather than become tangled up in theological discussions, I've turned to a scientific discipline to handle this technique. God is still in His heaven, and we're using a portion of His creative energy to head for the peace and fulfillment which all religious teachings promise.

So, with this scientific approach, the mystic beings drop into the background, and with them go all the factors which some people seemed to find frightening about these matters.

Your miracles will occur in perfectly "natural" ways. Maybe TV or the movies cause you to connote miracles with genies coming out of bottles in clouds of smoke, or flashes of lightning and echoing peals of thunder at the midnight crossroads, while owls shriek and bats skitter over abandoned graveyards.

Thank heavens for science! Those eerie scenarios belong in another age, and even when they are worked correctly, they're very difficult to carry out. Try asking your friendly local pharmacist for an eye of newt or an ounce of bat's blood!

When I refer to Acupineology miracles, I want you to realize that just because something great happens to you without puffs of green smoke and ghostly voices, the miracle is no less miraculous—and it's a good deal less scary!

Using Your Digital Activators

The miracles brought by Acupineology happen by what some people choose to call coincidence. That's an excellent label. Others may refer to good fortune or lucky chances.

Call it what you will, when Acupineology starts working for you, changes will take place that will bring you joy and happiness. Call them coincidence, lucky breaks, or miracles—just savor them, bask in them, and become one of this world's favored few.

The Expansive Touch of Jupiter Brings You Unlimited Cash and Possessions

The first digital activator we will examine closely is firmly connected with your pectoral field, and employs Jupiter techniques to delightfully enhance your material and cash status.

The *Jupiter gesture, Jupiter connection,* and *Jupiter massage* are keys to abundance, and when they are used at the appropriate times in conjunction with your daily iso-bionic energy workout they can banish debts forever, enable you to indulge your whims in buying whatever you fancy, and allow you to build up your security as if you'd suddenly fallen heir to a productive oil well.

In fact, Jupiter techniques can be better than being an oil baron in these uncertain times. Oil wells can dry up, invaders can steal your rights to the royalties, or some other fuel could be discovered that might erode your profits.

Iso-bionic energy is not concerned with world trading conditions. The energy is always there to be used, and it flows strongly no matter what the stock market is doing, enabling you to take advantage of reigning conditions to bring yourself the maximum possible benefits in the best and most profitable areas available at the time when you're using the energy.

The Expansive Touch of Jupiter

**POWER UNLIMITED
FROM THE JUPITER GESTURE**

Many times in your life you're placed in a position where the decision of one single person affects whether you sink or swim, moneywise.

Typically, you may be facing a loan officer who is going to either grant you a loan or turn thumbs down on your application. Or perhaps you're in the boss's office, asking for a raise that will decide whether you can continue to pay the rent as well as buy a few groceries. If you get the loan or the raise, you can breathe easily. If your request is refused, you could end up on the streets, homeless and facing destitution.

Innumerable situations like these arise during one's life, and the *Jupiter gesture* can swing the results in your favor.

Place your left forefinger (Jupiter finger) on the Jupiter mount at the base of your right forefinger. Wrap your left thumb and little finger comfortably around your right wrist.

Bend the second and third fingers of your left hand (Saturn and Sun fingers), and tuck them into your right palm.

Fold all of your right fingers, except the forefinger, gently down over your left fingers. Move your right thumb to the left and let it lie on your right second (Saturn) finger.

That took much longer to spell out than it does to actually perform. If you follow these instructions step by step, you'll find that your hands are in a perfectly natural position, especially if you lay your

The Expansive Touch of Jupiter

hands in your lap, or rest your elbows on the arms of a chair, on a desk, or on a table in front of you.

The gesture may appear to be innocuous, but the lines of force you're stimulating are titanic in their power. Find time during a crucial financial interview to make and hold that gesture for as long as possible.

Obviously, you would be unable to sign papers with your Jupiter gesture assembled. So take it apart when you need to, and put it together again at the next convenient opportunity.

Do not make a "big deal" about holding the gesture. Put it together only when it might seem natural for you to do so. If you sit or stand with your hands persistently locked together, your interviewer may think you're a trifle odd, and that could be a strike against you in his or her positive decision.

Iso-bionic energy is indeed ultimately powerful and can work miracles for you, but there's no sense in stacking the deck against yourself and giving the energy extra opposition to overcome.

The Jupiter gesture will amaze you with its efficiency. Use it relatively sparingly. It is designed for use at critical points in your financial state. Employ this gesture when you know that your future security is on the line, hanging on the decision of the influential person you are facing.

Calling on this potent technique when you're merely trying to float a loan from your spouse so that you can go out for an evening of bowling, or putting the bite on a friend to get ten bucks to gamble on the numbers, is not the name of this game. That would be like using a steam hammer to crack a walnut.

The Expansive Touch of Jupiter

Important, large-scale money dealings, such as buying or selling your house or business, or similar deals where dollars run into the hundreds or thousands (or millions), are where the Jupiter gesture slips smoothly into high gear and brings you success. In fact, it seems the bigger the sum involved, the better the Jupiter gesture works.

ATTRACTING RICH PARTNERS WITH THE JUPITER CONNECTION

This technique is strictly down-to-earth. The *Jupiter connection* can be used to attract rich partners, and that applies to business or personal matters. If you're looking for love and affection, turn to the Pollex contacts in Acu-Key 4. Jupiter is purely concerned with bringing you money by the carload, but it carries no gilt-edged guarantee of emotional harmony.

Having made that point clear, here is how you can put the Jupiter connection together. For the sake of propriety, let's assume that you've been granted the option on a business deal which you know is going to make a bundle in the future.

All you lack is a partner with the necessary cash to float this treasure trove. Maybe you have someone in mind whom you would like to co-sign with you. Or perhaps you have no one in view. Several "possibles" may exist.

You're certainly going to have to make some kind of sales pitch to someone, in order to persuade them to lay their wampum on the line.

You may do that face to face, by letter, or by telephone, or you may even have someone else act

The Expansive Touch of Jupiter

as your agent to do the selling for you. Just possibly, especially if you don't know anyone with that kind of money, you may run an advertisement in a newspaper, inviting interested parties to invest in your sure thing.

VcToria Comments: *Nowadays we would use e-mail, social media, fax etc.*

Sooner or later, you will know if you're dealing with a male or a female. Once you know the sex of your rich potential partner, you can start performing the Jupiter connection to ensure that the deal will be sewn up satisfactorily and profitably for you.

At the end of your daily iso-bionic energy workout, which is explained in detail in Acu-Key 9, spend about 60 seconds making the Jupiter connection.

Start it on the day after you know whom you're trying to influence, and continue it daily until the deal goes through and the partnership is signed, sealed, and delivered, or established firmly in some other significant way.

Here's how it goes. Hold your left hand up with the palm facing you, fingers straight and pointing to the right. Place your right hand, with the fingers straight and pointing to the left, on your left palm so that your right finger tips touch your left wrist. Naturally, your left finger tips will touch your right wrist, on the underside.

Start sliding your hands apart until your right forefinger (Jupiter finger) is touching:

a) The mount of the Moon on your left hand, if you're dealing with a female.

The Expansive Touch of Jupiter

    b) The mount of the Sun, if your future partner is a male.

    c) The plain of Uranus, if perchance you're in any doubt about the sex of your partner.

When your right forefinger is touching the correct mount or plain, you'll find that your left Jupiter finger will automatically make contact with the same mount on your right palm.

Close your eyes and hold that pose for about a minute, running thoughts through your mind of the fantastic profits that are going to accrue from the upcoming partnership.

Make these thoughts clear and precise, as if you already have control of hundreds of thousands of dollars, and more greenbacks are cascading into your joint bank account every minute of the day.

Then open your eyes, break the connection, and go about your business.

JUPITER MASSAGE MAKES SURE YOU'RE THE ONE WHO WINS

Jupiter massage puts your iso-bionic energy in top shape to handle any competitive situation which hinges on money or possessions.

Whatever you're selling or buying, you'll get the best possible bargain when you stimulate your Jupiter lines of force in your pectoral field with this massage technique.

As with the Jupiter gesture, this hand posture is unobtrusive and can be carried out in the presence of other people without arousing comment.

The Expansive Touch of Jupiter

But, to repeat a previously expressed idea, you should not continue with the massage if it is likely to earn you sideways glances. If you're offered a cigarette or coffee, stop the massage and accept the offered item. If you need to find something in your pocket or purse, reach for it and resume the massage only when convenient.

This incredible luck stimulator is no more complicated than any other technique in this book, but the results are out of all proportion to the effort involved on the physical plane.

With your hands together naturally on your knees, on your thighs, or in your lap, tuck your right thumb into your left hand, so that your thumb tip presses firmly on your left mount of Jupiter (base of forefinger). Your right mount of Venus will be touching your left mount of the Moon, and your right fingers will lie neatly over the back of your left hand.

Make sure your right forefinger (Jupiter) is resting with its tip on the knuckle of your left forefinger. Squeeze your right thumb and forefinger gently, and you'll be holding your left mount of Jupiter in a pincer grip.

Start to massage your right thumb in a small circle, round and round, feeling the flesh of your left mount of Jupiter moving under the massage.

Move the thumb clockwise or counterclockwise, whichever feels more comfortable. You may reverse the direction whenever you wish.

Perform this for up to a full minute throughout the period in which your luck is on the line.

That's the complete Jupiter massage. Just a small tip: If someone should notice your massage and make some comment, reply with a casual remark about sore knuckles or keeping your hands in shape for bowling, golf, or whatever. Do not blow your cover by telling your companion or opponent that you're a step ahead of the game with a fully charged pectoral field backed up by stimulated Jupiter lines of force which are swinging things your way.

THE JUPITER CONNECTION PERFORMANCE HAS BEEN FOLLOWED BY HEALING

Note: The following technique cannot be claimed as a cure, nor is it intended to be a substitute for conventional medical therapy. See your physician for any condition requiring medical treatment, and follow his or her recommendations and prescriptions.

The above important notice does not downgrade iso-bionic energy in the least. Nevertheless, I strongly recommend that you follow that advice. Jupiter connection usage has indeed been followed by apparent miracles of healing and increased vitality, but for me to tell you to rely solely on iso-bionic energy to rejuvenate your body would be unethical, and in certain cases possibly dangerous.

The hazard could arise if you have, for instance, a chronic condition which is being held in check by regular medication. If you suddenly abandon the treatment and turn to iso-bionic energy to bring you back to health, the change could be too much for your already weakened body. While you are bringing your energy fields up to full strength, your body

The Expansive Touch of Jupiter

could react to the withdrawal of medication, and you might end up sicker than ever.

A case illustrating that point occurred in Montreal, Canada, and concerned a young boy who was diabetic.

His daily shots of insulin were keeping the disease in check, and he was able to lead close to a normal life.

Then his mother took him to a "faith healer." This type of psychic healing is effective in many cases, and authentic examples seem to closely resemble the application of iso-bionic energy, where the healer feeds vitality into the sick person's body to enable the natural healing process to take place.

Unfortunately, the mother of the diabetic boy took the faith healer's advice to "cease using insulin at once, because the healing energies are making excess sugar flow out of the boy's finger tips."

That is a direct quote from the court evidence which came to light after the boy had gone into a diabetic coma and died. The healer was charged with practicing medicine without a license.

This tragic case is not one to scare you. It merely gives you a few facts to guide you in a confusing area.

I have no doubt that the boy's death could have been prevented if the insulin shots had been maintained. Then, provided the healer was not one of the fakes and charlatans whose shameful and illegal pitches for clients disgrace the advertising pages of the yellow press, her God-given healing powers might have assisted the orthodox medical treatment to bring the boy back to health.

VcToria Comments: *Today we see such advertising on the internet and social media pages. My Father, with his words of 'yellow press,' was referring to the phone books that were distributed in the 1970's.*

That's the vital key to using Jupiter connections—or any other form of natural energy—where poor health exists. Use them as assists to your doctor's efforts on your behalf.

So, having perhaps frightened you with an awful example of the dangers of gullibility, I will now show you the right way to do it, along with any treatment your medical advisor recommends.

As you're already aware, Jupiter is connected most strongly with material things, those you can see and touch. So the Jupiter connection is on record as operating most convincingly where poor physical health is concerned.

If your problem is something a psychiatrist is treating, the Jupiter connections, although they will not aggravate the condition, will not be operating in their most efficient realm.

The physical act of carrying out the Jupiter connection is described a few pages back. You'll know which mount to touch, depending on whether you're male or female: Sun for men and Moon for women. If, as is becoming more prevalent these days, you're in doubt about your sexual preference and your masculinity or femininity, the plain of Uranus is your contact point.

The Expansive Touch of Jupiter

Using the Jupiter connection for acquiring a rich partner, and for helping yourself to get well, differs only in the time and place of making the connection.

In Acu-Key 8, you'll find out how to identify the "up" dates of your solar systemic nodes, times when destiny is on your side.

When you've found your systemic node "up" dates, you'll be ready to apply the Jupiter connection to your bodily state.

I have purposely included the solar systemic nodes and how to discover them toward the end of this book. You'll get the greatest benefit if you absorb this whole work from cover to cover before trying any of the techniques. Skipping along, reading the bits which attract you, and trying to extract unrelated scraps of Acupineology, without taking the time to understand the whole concept, is very likely to lead you to write me a letter asking, "What am I doing wrong? My iso-bionic energy isn't working too well."

VcToria Comments: *Since you cannot write to my Dad I would assume you would e-mail or private message me. If you truly have questions please post them on the forums on Face Book so that all may read and understand them instead of directly contacting me. I keep a forum that can be 'searched' with Geof Gray-Cobb. Read on.*

Acupineology is a complete, self-contained, life-changing discipline. All of the recommended exercises are necessary to success for the average person. Daily application and practice are needed to make it work, except in exceptional cases where

The Expansive Touch of Jupiter

Acupineology has been found to work its miracles almost instantly. Most people will find that regular application is the secret to making these techniques work effectively.

With that suggestion behind us, let us proceed toward influencing your physical health.

From the solar systemic nodes explanation in Acu-Key 8, you will obtain the dates on which your iso-bionic energy is naturally flowing most strongly. These are the periods when you should make every effort to apply healing assistance with the Jupiter connection.

It can, of course, be performed at any time, but the node times are those you should mark in your diary as being slanted toward greatest vitality improvement.

Perform the Jupiter connection for 60 seconds after you lie down to sleep, on the night before your "up" solar systemic node period begins. Make the connection again before rising the next day, applying it for another 60 seconds.

While you're making the connection, close your eyes, relax, and imagine how you will feel when you are well. On no account tell yourself anything like, "This Jupiter connection will help my sore back to get better." Naming the malady in your mind tends to maintain it, instead of healing it. So, pretend, for 60 seconds each time that your sickness is cured.

When the malady has receded and you're in blooming health again, do not fuss about whether your doctor cured you or whether the Jupiter connection had anything to do with it. If you claim that you were cured by iso-bionic energy that will

The Expansive Touch of Jupiter

provoke your doctor, who has been using the best of his or her skills to help you.

Be happy and move on to your next miracle. What's gone is gone, and the time you spend trying to clearly establish why something happened is wasted time which could be better used to shape your future, instead of fruitlessly reviewing your past.

JUPITER CONNECTIONS SHOW YOU EXACTLY HOW TO WIN AT NUMBERS, LOTTERIES, OR SWEEPSTAKES

I've said these things before, in many different ways, in countless articles, lectures, and books. You may never have heard me express this idea, however, so I'll repeat myself.

If I knew a sure-fire, gold-plated, guaranteed secret for winning at gambling, I'd do two things. First, I'd write a book telling you how to do it. Then, I'd do it myself and put my feet up.

And that would probably be a mistake for me. My astrology chart says that I have many years to go yet on this earthly plane, and I'll die in harness, probably still hammering at this faithful old typewriter, trying to pass on my latest understanding of this wonderful world we live in.

Truthfully, I'm too busy having a good time to really pour myself into making a financial killing by means of natural energies. Maybe one day, just to prove a point, I'll join the other people I know who have won big by using their luck cycles and esoteric know-how.

The Expansive Touch of Jupiter

VcToria Comments: *This original book was published in 1980. True to his astrology chart he did not pass till May 12th 2009. True to his words, he was still pushing out his words via books. His last book 'Twist of Fate' was published in 2008. However, computers had come to pass by then and he was hammering away on them, no doubt with great delight that he had a 'delete' button rather than that white stuff you needed to erase a letter while using a typewriter.*

I do not have the rights to Twist of Fate as Shiffer is still publishing it and has the rights as of now [2019]. There is a mistake in the mathematical area in this book as by then Dad was showing his age and obviously it was not edited correctly. But he did predict that he would be doing his passion till late in life. He chose not to gamble.

One thing I know for sure is that winning at gambling depends on luck. You can shave the odds by studying form and handicapping, analyzing the run of playing cards, knowing the chances of rolling a seven, or a thousand other tips and wrinkles beloved of the average speculator.

But, when it comes to the crunch, if Lady Luck fails to smile on you, you join the losers bemoaning your malignant fate. The Jupiter connection definitely helps. You make this connection when destiny is smiling on you as much as she's likely to at the time when you're going to make your play, buy a ticket, or however else you intend to break the bank.

These times are exactly the same as those used for helping yourself to heal, which were described a couple of pages back.

The Expansive Touch of Jupiter

Your strongest periods of iso-bionic energy flow are derived from the "up" solar systemic nodes instructions in Acu-Key 8.

If your big gambling day is fixed by the date on which the race or game is being held, select the latest three-day systemic node "up" period which occurs before the date you're going to speculate.

If you're free to pick and choose your investment time, gamble at any time during an "up" solar systemic node period, carrying out your Jupiter connection on the night before the period starts, and repeating the connection on the next two nights.

That gives you the "when" of it. The "where" is the same as for self-healing: in bed. The critical difference is that you make the Jupiter connection exactly as described for healing, be the very last thing you do as you drift into the sleep state. There is no requirement for you to make the connection again upon awakening.

You'll notice, when you've worked out your solar systemic nodes that you have a maximum of five three-day "up" periods each year when Dame Fortune is on your team.

You'll also discover at least three, and maybe four, periods of "down" nodes, when no gamble is likely to go right for you.

Aside from those dates, there's no way of discovering whether or not you're likely to be lucky, unless you retain the professional services of an experienced astrologer, who is deeply into this method of calculating good fortune times. That's a long and tedious process, and at the going rates for

The Expansive Touch of Jupiter

a really expert job, you could be faced with expenses close to a thousand dollars. That's a lot of scratch, especially considering that no ethical astrologer will give you a warranty that you'll be in the right place at the right time to draw the greatest benefit from your good fortune period.

VcToria Comments: *Due to computers now being able to program an astrology chart with transits, you may, if you like ask her to offer you some dates. See her web store on* **www.alternativeuniverse.ca** *to order a full chart or simple the 'lucky gambling chart.' The cost is much lower than was asked for in the 1980's.*

Now that you've made your Jupiter connection and drifted into slumber, we come to the "how" of the method.

You're going to *dream* your winning bet. No kidding—it will be a clear, precise directive, telling you which animal, which lottery ticket seller, which bingo hall, which team *and* the points spread, or whatever else you need to know to make the big killing.

That's what you'll wake up with, and if you take my advice you'll write it down before it disappears from your memory while you're sipping your first morning coffee.

What if you find no dream in your memory as you wake up? The most likely reason for this is that you had the dream, among the eight or nine other dreams you have every night, but it failed to stay in your memory. This is a sure sign that you may have skimped a bit on your daily iso-bionic energy workout, or in some other way you neglected to give

The Expansive Touch of Jupiter

your iso-bionic energy the maximum chance to get working for you.

Another possible reason for the lack of recall of a dream is that you may have gone to bed under the befuddling influences of alcohol or drugs. That tends to muddy the waters in your dreams, and can prevent you from recalling details clearly.

In one respect, the cure is simple. Stay off the booze or other mind-bending stuff for 24 hours before you make the connection. However, that does *not* apply if you're taking prescription drugs. As I stated firmly earlier, follow your doctor's orders or else you could be storing up problems for yourself.

The point here, obscure as it may seem to you at the moment, is that if you succumbed to a bout of disease and have had to visit the doctor or a hospital, then your iso-bionic energy is at a low ebb for some reason. If you're low on energy to keep you well, it's unlikely that there will be any spare energy to help you win.

If you have a chronic condition which requires constant medication to keep it in check, your case is different. Your body will have a tolerance for any drugs you're being given, and your iso-bionic energy will be as powerful as that of a person who is totally healthy.

If you fail to wake up with a useful dream, and you went to bed clear-headed and apparently fully charged from your previous daily energy workout, it may be that iso-bionic energy is telling you something else important.

Absence of a winning dream can mean that, although you're in a lucky period, it's not lucky

The Expansive Touch of Jupiter

enough to hit first place in the fortune stakes. You may be planning to bet with a bookie whose iso-bionic energy happens to be more topped up than yours. So your on-the-nose bets get beaten out of the money by a nose, while your show bets miss being placed.

At times like these, your full house gets clobbered by a royal flush, you get four numbers right but they're in the wrong order, or you experience some of the hundred and one other frustrations which put you close to the money, but let someone else carry off the loot. That's a very good time to keep your money in your purse!

If you do wake up with a clear and incisively directional dream on how to win, act on it. People who win consistently, day after day, are very rare, so you need to ride your luck when it's ripe.

I have a letter on file from a young man who dreamed about three horses winning on the following day. He wrote them down, then got distracted by a pretty face and seductive words, and spent the day in bed with his girlfriend. His dream selections romped home, but he had not wagered on them. He's been bemoaning his bad luck ever since, and he says that he has never dreamed another winner.

We could surmise that iso-bionic energy is prepared to show you the ways to win, but if you choose to ignore them, the energy will turn to some other way to make you contented.

Yes, you can win with Jupiter connections.

VcToria Comments: *I have removed all the testimonials as many requested this. However, know* *that with these books, by being re-printed, the cost of the originals have now dropped drastically. If you still wish to read the testimonials you may also purchase the one's printed in 1980 on line through second hand book sellers.*

HOW TO PRESERVE YOUR NEW-FOUND WEALTH

Whether it's the gamble of the stock market, speculation in the business world, or the "investment" of gambling, you're all set to clean up the next time Lady Luck smiles your way.

But, once you've gotten yourself a bank balance to rival the Rockefellers, are you going to be able to hang on to it?

It's a proven fact that a high proportion of people who suddenly hit a jackpot are so stunned by the change that they fritter away their money and their lives, often ending up exactly where they started from, destitute and hurt, sometimes after only a few short months.

With Acupineology on your side, there's no reason why you should follow that unfortunate path. Even when you've built yourself up to the peak you've dreamed about, keep the Acupineology routines going.

For instance, make your major investments during your solar systemic node "up" periods, and hold back during the "downs." Keep the freeloaders and con artists at arm's length. They'll flock your way as you get richer, and you'd do well to repel them with iso-bionic energy techniques.

That's a brief piece of friendly advice. The world is full of "money vampires" who want to suck you dry of your cash and assets. You may have met a few already!

So, use Acupineology to hang on to your inspired gains, and when any creepy con person tries to take advantage of you, see right through the scheme with Acupineology and get out from under in a hurry. Acu-Key 5 presents a number of powerful techniques for this. But first, peruse and apply the methods in Acu-Key 4 to find peace of mind and love.

Achieve True Peace, Freedom, and Love with the Amazing Pollex Techniques

At the end of Acu-Key 3, I touched briefly on the attitudes of some negative people with whom you may come in contact during your life. You've no doubt already found out how unpleasant some people can be.

This section offers you an effective method of keeping such people under control so that they cannot hurt you.

REACTIONS AND EMOTIONS

Pardon me for presenting this explanatory preamble before handing you the whole technique. The following is essential to your understanding of what these techniques will achieve for you.

You should recognize an important feature of any tight spot you get into, or any situation you find painful. The root cause of the discomfort, are the actions and reactions of all the people involved, *including yourself.*

Consider what a splendid advantage you would gain if you could unerringly have control over these reactions and emotions. Given that ability, you would have a fantastic vehicle to turn indifference into love, opposition into acceptance, pain into pleasure, and to vitally convert the unpleasant into contentment.

That's precisely what these *pollex techniques* can bring you, besides offering some other specific energy enhancements which you'll find ultimately useful and valuable in your emotional and physical life.

BREAK ALL RESTRICTIONS WITH POLLEX-INSPIRED WILLPOWER

Anyone who studies palmistry learns very early on that the human thumb is the part of the hand connected with willpower.

Moving with that concept into the science of Acupineology, we find that the iso-bionic energy connected with the thumb (Pluto) is indeed mentally oriented. The lines of force which flow through your psinic, pectoral, and umbilical fields have unsuspected effects on the way you react to circumstances, and the ways people react to you.

This is where Figure 2, on page 56, is used again. Using the table to identify the life areas needing attention, we assign your right thumb as the contact digit, while your left palm, fingers, and thumb are the areas where you complete vital energy circuits.

Much of what we are about to accomplish with this technique has its beginnings deep within your mind and body as the appropriate lines of force knit life-changing webs of iso-bionic energy in and around you.

The Expansive Touch of Jupiter

Please read and comprehend this next section carefully. It is a vital key to finding peace of mind in any and all situations destiny brings to you.

POLLEX CONTACT SHIELDS NEGATIVITY

The way you feel about a person or a situation depends on how you react. The particular person or circumstance is merely a trigger which prompts you to make some response. If that response is fear, anger, or confusion, you feel tensions and discomfort.

Let me give you a simple example, to better illustrate my meaning. Let us assume that you're in a room, sitting opposite another person, a stranger whom you've never seen before.

Imagine that the other person starts to pull ugly faces at you, and then proceeds to criticize your appearance, your accomplishments, your family, and your background.

Quite predictably, you'll begin to feel angry or scared. Depending on your psychology, you might walk out of the room, shaking with fear and anger, or you might take a swing at the stranger and give him a fat lip.

Allow me now to add a couple of other things to this imagined scenario. Assume, for the sake of this example, that your ears are stuffed with wax plugs, so that you're unable to hear a thing. In addition, your eyes are covered with soft wads of cotton, so that you cannot see anything.

The stranger opposite you goes through the same routine, grimacing at you and making hurtful remarks. You neither see nor hear this, so you're able to sit calmly and coolly as the unheard and unseen tirade pass you by.

You do not become scared or angry, because you have experienced nothing to which you can react. Yet, the same conditions existed before when you experienced the verbal and visual assault and got uptight.

The difference is that you did not react the second time. The wax and cotton were blocking the incoming stimulation, so you felt totally unpressured and unthreatened.

Now, what if you had a simple Acupineology technique which accomplished the same goal as the cotton pads and wax plugs, *without* making you temporarily blind and deaf? What a powerful shield that would be to protect you from turmoil when life gets pressured and aggravating!

Pollex contact gives you that ultimate weapon. Using this technique, you'll find that you can resist the upwelling trauma under any condition you may come across, and that puts you in a state of peace and harmony which you'll only understand fully when you have experienced it.

The method consists of simply having your charged-up iso-bionic energy flow from your right thumb to your left palm.

Whenever you feel pressured, make a quick analysis of the situation. As the first knots of tension begin in your stomach, as you feel the first quiver of apprehension or surge of anger, identify what is bothering you.

The Expansive Touch of Jupiter

Decide which mount on your left palm is identified with the situation, and press your right thumb firmly onto that mount.

You've now made your pollex contact, and the results will be remarkable. You will feel the early tensions drain away, and you'll be able to face up to whatever fate has in store for you, calmly, firmly, and decisively. The following examples will put you on the right track.

Aggravating husband

Your husband is bugging, and you're about to lose your cool. The mount of the Sun at the base of your third finger rules male partners. {See Figure 2 on page 56}

Press your right thumb into the left mount of the Sun, and no matter how your spouse is behaving, you will feel the tensions leave you, and you'll be able to rationally dispose of the impending battle.

Aggravating wife

The situation and pollex contact is identical to the above aggravating husband case, but the mount to press is the mount of the Moon, as shown in Figure 2.

Intimidating official

You are facing a lawyer or a bureaucrat who is scaring you with veiled threats. Your right thumb presses your mount of Jupiter. The result is that you are able to meet your tormentor point for point and salvage the best from the confrontation, instead of rolling over and being trampled on.

The Expansive Touch of Jupiter

Stage fright

You have to make a speech before an audience, and it scares you witless. The mount of the Moon (public influence, as shown in Figure 2) is your contact point. Press and you will confidently make the impact of your career.

Annoying children

Are your kids acting up? The mount of Mercury, contacted by your right thumb, will bring you the sanity, calmness, and strength to deal with them firmly and fairly.

Afraid to speak out

Are you scared to speak up for yourself? Do you need some courage and moderate aggression? The mount of Mars, contacted by your right thumb, brings reserves of bravery and tenacity you were unaware you had.

Overstayed welcome

When you wish that a tedious neighbor would finish her coffee and interminable gossip and go home, when you wish to *eliminate* someone's presence, your right thumb is pressed on the top joint of your left thumb, bringing Pluto energy to bear, and giving you the right words to say. If that neighbor doesn't stand up and depart within three minutes, you need to do more iso-bionic energy charging!

USE SEVERAL MOUNTS IF NECESSARY

The above examples are merely a few of the endless possibilities of gain with pollex contact.

The Expansive Touch of Jupiter

There's no need to fuss about whether you've pressed the correct mount. In fact, if you prefer to cover more than one base, move your thumb around from mount to mount, staying on each one for about 15 seconds.

For example, your boss might be threatening you with punishment and you want to protect yourself. In succession, press your right thumb to the mounts of Sun (employer), Saturn (punishment), and Jupiter (protection).

The energy obeys your mental command. As you contact the mounts, think about what you wish to have happen. Call up a clear picture of the desired end result of your action, and iso-bionic energy will do the rest, provided you follow through and do or say the right things which automatically come to mind.

Your iso-bionic energy fields lead to your personal harmony. So, when you channel the energy, it prompts you to select the most peaceful or constructive path at that time.

I've anticipated your final question. What if you feel tense, angry, confused, or depressed, and for the life of you there seems to be no good reason?

Hold your right thumb firmly onto the plain of Uranus, the planet of surprise, the unexpected, and change. Hold the pressure, as with all other pollex contacts, for a minimum of 15 seconds.

You can think of the plain of Uranus as your ace in the hole. Whenever you cannot reach a decision about which mount to contact, go for the plain of Uranus.

The Expansive Touch of Jupiter

It sets up powerful change influences which can catapult you into calmer conditions.

POLLEX MASSAGE POINTS BRING SURGING NATURAL ENERGY

Now we come to a delicate subject which I will cover in some detail because I receive so many letters and queries about it. I have treated this in as clinical a manner as possible, but if you are offended by sexual technique instructions, please pass over this section.

This *pollex massage* technique requires you to touch the bare skin of another person, probably in private or intimate surroundings. *On no account must you force any of these massage techniques on anyone, or take them by surprise.* In the strict legal sense, when you touch someone else without their express permission, if they object strongly enough, you could find yourself the subject of an assault charge.

I hasten to add that I'm not going to suggest that you make any obscene gestures with pollex massage. Yet, a few people are insecure enough to become scared and disturbed when another person touches them, and should you make contact with such a paranoid person, you might find yourself having to work hard at other Acupineology techniques to struggle out from under a sticky situation.

As a general rule, except when you're performing this massage on yourself, the person you're operating on must be what has become known as a "consenting adult," and will often be your spouse or lover.

The Expansive Touch of Jupiter

With these cautions firmly stated, we can proceed to the crux of this technique.

The *pollex massage points* are aids in clearing two of the greatest obstacles to sexual harmony: impotence, the inability of a male to achieve or maintain an erection, and frigidity, the inability of a female to fully respond to a sexual encounter.

The field we are going to stimulate is the umbilical field. These techniques work with greatest efficiency when bare flesh-to-flesh contact is made.

Umbilical massage point

Bare the lower abdomen, and place both thumbs gently on the navel. Slide the hands three inches downward, toward the genitals, keeping the thumbs together.

At that point, press the thumbs firmly into the abdomen and rotate them in a small circle, maintaining steady pressure.

After about 60 seconds of this massage, move the hands slightly up the body so that the forefingers make contact with the same point on the abdomen. Repeat 60 seconds of pressure and circular movement, Finally, do the same with the second (Saturn) fingers.

When making the small massaging circles, do not slide the thumb or fingers across the skin. Make the flesh move under the circular pressure. Try it once and you'll understand the technique.

This massage should be carried out daily, and also before sexual intercourse, as long as impotence or frigidity persists. The technique can easily be done on yourself or a partner.

In either case, the person being treated should be lying on his or her back, relaxed and comfortable.

VcToria Comments: *If you are standing behind the persons head and working from that position then the hand movements are correct. If you are standing at the base of the person the hand movements would be opposite. If self-administered the hand movements are correct.*

Lower back massage points

This massage cannot easily be self-administered. You can do it to a partner or have it done to you.

The individual being treated should lie face down, relaxed and calm. Bare the lower back.

Press both thumbs gently into the upper buttocks, and locate the bulge of the pelvic bone on either side of the spine. Move the thumbs toward each other until they are three inches apart, one thumb on each side of the spine. Press firmly and rotate both thumbs in small circles for 60 seconds.

The hands should be open, with the fingers lying naturally on the flesh of the waist or upper buttocks.

The greatest benefits will be gained when this massage is carried out daily, and prior to any physical sexual involvements.

Shoulder pollex massage

This massage is for use on females only. It will arouse the sexual appetite and help to alleviate frigidity. Males will gain little sexual benefit from the technique, apart from a relief of tension.

The Expansive Touch of Jupiter

The woman should be seated. Stand behind her and bare her shoulders. Imagine a vertical line drawn up from each of her nipples, crossing the collar bone on the way up, and arriving at a point on the major muscle which runs across the top of the shoulder.

With your thumb behind (closest to you) and your forefinger over the top of the muscle, squeeze gently, lifting a section of the flesh and muscle. Use one hand on each shoulder, lifting simultaneously with both hands.

Release the pressure then squeeze again. Repeat the massage, continuing to squeeze and release every two or three seconds.

Gradually increase the pressure with each squeeze, asking the woman to tell you when it hurts. When she says you're squeezing hard enough, slacken the pressure a trifle, and continue with the regular squeezing at that pressure for about a minute longer, or two minutes total, whichever is the longer.

This shoulder pollex massage has helped many females to reach new heights of enjoyment in sexual intercourse.

POLLEX PRESSURE POINT HOLDS PAIN AT BAY

In the introduction to this book, you may recall that I mentioned that pain is a warning that something is wrong within your body. The technique I am offering you here can subdue pain, but you should always seek to cure the cause of the pain.

The Expansive Touch of Jupiter

If you have a toothache, this *pollex pressure point* will keep the pain under control. It is unlikely, though, that it will remove the *cause*, so you should visit your dentist at the earliest opportunity.

You should recognize this pressure point as an emergency, interim resource to keep you comfortable until you can reach medical treatment. It is nothing more than that, but it is extremely useful and comforting when you're miles away from a bottle of aspirin.

The pressure point is down in the soft flesh between your left thumb and forefinger, close to the mount of Mars.

Hold your left hand with the fingers relaxed and fairly straight. Tuck the top of your right thumb down between the left thumb and forefinger. Grip your hands together and press the right thumb down hard, pushing toward the wrist.

VcToria Comments: *Where he says 'grip your hands together' may confuse some. Just close the hands together as if in prayer. Now bend the fingers down in-between each other and make sure the right thumb is resting between the forefinger and thumb of the left hand. Press down hard.*

Almost at once any pain, anywhere in your body, will start to recede, and even the most agonizing distress can be subdued to a bearable level. Continue the pressure until the pain has either disappeared, as it most likely will, or until it reaches a lesser level and does not seem to be diminishing any further.

Release the pressure slowly, and observe if the pain returns or grows stronger. If it does, perform the thumb pressure again.

Continue with this until the pain stops worrying you. But get medical help soon. I repeat: *Any pain that is strong or persistent needs medical diagnosis at the earliest opportunity.* Please do not use this pressure point to postpone needed health care.

BANISH FEARS AND PHOBIAS WITH THIS POLLEX CONTACT

As with all these health care techniques, I again advise a caution. If you need, or are under, psychiatric care, do not abandon or postpone the treatment, simply because you find this pollex contact alleviates the mental condition.

This is a specific pollex contact which is precisely the same as one described earlier. The only difference is that the hands are reversed. This is simply because I've found that it works that way. It seems, in this particular case, that the energy flow is reversed.

Place your left thumb on the mount of Jupiter of your right hand. Tuck the left fingers behind the right hand, placing them across the tendons of the right hand. Squeeze gently, holding the pressure for about a minute. Release your grip and separate your hands.

If you have a longstanding phobia, such as a fear of the dark, or of insects, dogs, spiders, or a fear of anything, a daily workout with this pollex contact will see your fears grow less and finally vanish.

In any situation of danger where you feel suddenly lost and scared, quickly make this pollex contact and feel a new sureness flood through your mind and body, bringing clear thinking and the right instinctive reactions to get you out of trouble and save the situation.

ALL NEGATIVE CONDITIONS DISSOLVE WHEN YOU USE POLLEX CONTACTS

I have done my best to make pollex contacts unobtrusive, so that you can use them at almost any time without attracting undue attention to yourself. Of course, the exceptions are the sexually-oriented massage techniques. Those, I trust, you will perform in privacy, not in a public place.

The whole concept of pollex contacts is to erect a powerful barrier against pain, turmoil, manipulation, fear, pressure, and repression. You need suffer no more humiliation from more aggressive or unethical people. Pollex contacts enable you to sail calmly through any situation, picking up available benefits on the way.

With regular usage, you'll transform yourself into a new person. Negative conditions that used to have you wound up like a bowstring will no longer aggravate you. Your life will therefore open up like a spring flower, and you'll be free to follow your own desires and destiny to the contented peak which is the natural state for all human beings.

Moon Techniques Quickly Bring Vast Profits

Much of our journey together, unraveling the facts of Acupineology, has been concerned with tangible things, either those you can see and touch, or mental effects whose results can be perceived in the actions and reactions of yourself and other people.

Now we take an interesting step into the sphere of intangibles, the abstract, and the unseen and often unfelt part of our world.

Abstractions are frequently ideas or concepts. For example, "freedom" is an abstraction, something you cannot see or touch. "Liberty" is another abstraction, and so are "happiness" and "sadness."

None of these things can be handled or seen, but we're well aware that they exist. Abstract or not, we know when we're free, happy, or sad.

This aspect of Acupineology deals directly with abstractions, showing you how you can manipulate the mystic world of intangibles with *Moon techniques*. Here are easy ways to turn sadness into happiness, confinement into glorious freedom, oppression into control—all abstractions that are invisible and untouchable, but the benefits and profits resulting from their manipulation are most definitely material and enjoyable in the mundane world of money, assets, and tangible possessions.

CONFUSED? MOON MASSAGE MAKES EVERYTHING CLEAR

Sometimes we reach stages in our lives where we truly do not know which way to turn. Trying to peer into a dim and apparently troubled future, we wonder what step to take next.

Often, we have several alternatives open to us, and we can spend days and weeks pondering which choice to make. In that time, opportunities can disappear into thin air, bad situations can get worse, and our tendency can be to curl up into a tight ball of misery and do nothing, hoping that the negativity and turmoil will go away by themselves.

Ignoring problems and decisions rarely helps. Even a bad decision is better than no decision at all; at least it gets things moving, and brings some change. Our lives exist in the midst of change. Those of us who try to cling to the past tend to be the least happy. Adaptation and alteration are two key features for a contented life style.

Would you like to know, without a shadow of a doubt, the right thing to do for your own happiness? You're in luck: *Moon massage* will unerringly tell you, simply and quickly. There will be no more worrying about whether you should do this or that. Clear and precise decisions are given to you, backed by the knowledge that the path opening up is the most serene one possible at that time, and will lead you to peace and fulfillment.

You can control destiny with Moon massage

A little thought will show you that most of the things which make up your future and decide

Moon Techniques Quickly Bring Vast Profits

whether it will go well or ill are formed in abstract areas.

Decisions, ideas, and plans for action all happen in someone's mind. It may happen in your own mind, as you decide what you're going to do next. Or it may happen in the mind of someone else, who makes decisions that affect you just as strongly as if he or she had met you face to face and forced you to take some line of action.

This is precisely where Moon massage can work its wonders for you, shaping ideas and projects so that you are the prime beneficiary, making use of hidden levels of your mind which you might never have explored before to such magnificent effect.

Moon massage technique

As with the other aspects of Acupineology, the technique of Moon massage is simple in execution and startling in its towering sequels.

Sit or lie down comfortably, in private, as quietly as possible. Turn off the TV or radio and try to choose a time when outside noises are at their lowest level.

Hold your hands up in front of you, palms facing you, and put the edges of your palms together, pinkie touching pinkie.

Cup your hands a little, and turn the palms toward each other so that the mounts of Mercury, Neptune, and the Moon on one hand touch the same mounts on the other hand.

Begin a slow and easy up and down movement of one hand against the other. At each slide, the mount of Mercury on one hand will massage the other hand's mounts of Neptune and the Moon. Reverse the motion each time a mount of Mercury has moved fully down across the opposite mount of the Moon.

VcToria Comments: *This is easier to do if you picture yourself rubbing your hands up and down. Look at the map of your hand and it will make sense when you look at the placements of the Mount of Moon and Mount of Neptune.*

Close your eyes, relax, and move your hands up and down as described 50 times, counting the movements in your mind. Each up and down movement counts as one complete massage.

A glowing warmth will begin along the edges of your palms. You're stimulating your iso-bionic energy, bringing your umbilical field to a rolling boil. You may even feel the energy prickling or surging in your lower abdomen as the charge builds up.

When you're through, open your eyes, separate your hands some people vow that they hear a faint crackling of power as they do that—and do whatever you have to do next, whether it's an Acupineology exercise or some other mundane task.

Daily Moon massage, following your iso-bionic energy workout, does fascinating things to your thinking patterns, and the decisions of people who play important roles in your life.

When you are faced with a decision, you'll automatically do the right thing to bring harmony and progress to yourself in the *long view*. Note those last two words: iso-bionic energy pervades your whole universe, including your future as well as your here-and-now present life.

Moon Techniques Quickly Bring Vast Profits

The strong field you set up with Moon massage starts working to take you directly to happier pastures, sometimes along a path which may seem strange or illogical. Let go and let the umbilical field reshape your life. When you have time to look back, you'll realize that what seemed to be an odd happening a year ago was actually the trigger for a chain of events which led directly to your total ecstasy right now.

MAKE THE MOON CONTACT AND BECOME A SUPER-SNOOPER

Even though you will soon gain clear evidence that Moon massage is working for you to keep you ahead of the competition, vanquish your enemies, and turn your life into a bowl of cherries without any pits, it's sometimes useful to know what other people are up to. This *Moon contact* hands you that information on a platter, secretly and confidentially. You can then stop worrying about whether anyone is trying to get the better of you or damage you. You can also enjoy the reassuring sight of Moon massage swinging destiny your way, and laugh happily at the discomfort of your adversaries.

Moon contact technique

Carry out this Moon contact under the same relaxed and quiet conditions described for your Moon massage.

Open your left hand flat, and straighten your right second finger on your RIGHT hand (Saturn finger). Lay it across your left palm, with the finger tip touching the mount of Mars. The lower part of your finger, or possibly the mount of Saturn, will lie in contact with the mount of the Moon on your left palm.

Having made this contact, hold it there and relax your hands into your lap or onto your stomach or chest, whichever is most comfortable for you.

Close your eyes and think about the people you wish to know about. What happens next depends on which of three types of human brain you were born with.

Dr. W. Grey Walter explains this concept very clearly in his book, *The Living Brain*, but you do not need to read a copy of that fascinating book, which came out in paperback in 1963. I'll explain the necessary concepts to you.

Know your brain type

Dr. Walter found that people have distinctively different things happening in their minds when they are thinking. At one time it was believed that everyone experienced more or less the same sensations when using the imagination, but Dr. Walter proved otherwise.

About 67 people out of 100 think in "pictures." If you're one of that majority, when you read the words "green truck," a kind of mental movie of a green vehicle flashes through your mind. You actually "see" the truck, somewhere inside your head.

About 17 people in 100 go further than a simple flash of a passing truck. Reading "green truck," they not only visualize a brightly painted truck, but they also mentally sketch in the highway that it's running along, perhaps a radar trap around a curve ahead, the state of the weather, the time of year. If asked,

Moon Techniques Quickly Bring Vast Profits

they can probably name the driver, know what's going through his mind, and where he's heading. All of this takes place in the imagination, of course, but that's the way that type of brain operates.

The remaining people, 16 out of every 100, do not think in any kind of pictures. The words "green truck" do not bring even a flash of wheels or green into their minds. There's nothing wrong with this type of brain; the owner has just as efficient an imagination as the others described above. But no pictures arrive, merely a flow of words, numbers, concepts, and impressions connected with green trucks in general.

These people rarely recall their dreams, or else they have to work hard at remembering them the moment they awaken. The people in the 17 percent group, who think in very detailed pictures, invariably dream in glorious technicolor every night.

I am telling you this at some length because I've received enough letters on the subject for me to research the point. Many books, and mine are no exception, tell you to "make a picture in your mind." Or, you may be instructed to "imagine a TV screen, and see movies on it."

That's fine and dandy for the people who think in pictures, but ultimately frustrating for those who lack the "picture-making" type of brain. So, I've brought these facts to your attention so that you will know what to expect in the next step of the Moon contact.

It might be a good idea to read the foregoing section again, paying close attention to what appears in your mind as you read the words "green truck."

With the appended explanations, you'll know what type of brain you have.

Continued Moon contact technique

You have closed your eyes and turned your thoughts to your foes, rivals, or whomever. Stay relaxed and pay attention to whatever comes into your mind as your iso-bionic energy flows through the mounts which are in contact.

If you think in pictures, you will "see" what your opponents are doing at that time. If pictures are not part of your brain's data processing, you're possibly even better off. You'll "know" exactly what is going on, as a clear stream of words, facts, and ideas come cascading into your head.

Either way, you'll receive the data you need, and it takes no more than a minute to tune into this, once you've practiced the routine a few times daily.

The challenge for me is to express how this feels. In cold print, the best way I can express it is to say the thoughts coming from your Moon contact have a different mental "flavor" from that of your regular personal thoughts. Some people describe it as "listening in on a silent telephone." Others imply that they "look" into a different corner of their minds to pick up this useful flow of information.

You have opened up a hot line

How do you know this process is not just your imagination, a false fantasy dreamed up by your subconscious? At the outset, you can never be perfectly certain, and no amount of assurance that you have a clear, open line into the lives of someone else will totally convince you. But subsequent events

Moon Techniques Quickly Bring Vast Profits

will prove that you were not fantasizing. If you confidentially check out the facts you receive, you will soon be reassured of the genuine value of the method.

Once you can appreciate the startling clarity of Moon contact, you will find that the pictures, words, and ideas which came to you were literally true. You *did* open up a hot line to someone else. As they say, the proof of the pudding is in the eating, and you'll gain full confidence in Moon contact as soon as you have seen it operate with unerring accuracy a few times.

MOON CONNECTIONS LOCATE HIDDEN TREASURE

You may have heard of *dowsing*, the ancient art of locating water or buried objects by gifted people who walk around with a hazel twig which dips to earth when they're close to their unseen target.

Some people also call it *water witching*, and here you're about to discover a technique which makes you about four times better than most expert dowsers at locating hidden or lost objects.

This is a variation on another detection technique which has been around for centuries. You are going to add iso-bionic energy to enhance your accuracy and the speed of your results.

You may have used a pendulum at some time, either as a party game or more seriously in psychic work.

In essence, the pendulum technique requires you to tie a small weight, such as a finger ring or similar object, on the end of a thread or thin string about 10 inches (25.4 cm) long.

You hold the end of the string, allowing the weight to swing free. When you ask a question which has a yes or no answer, the pendulum "replies."

Moon connection adds an extra dimension to this recognized way of tapping the intangible levels of your mind and the world around you.

Make a pendulum as I have just described. Sit down at a table so that you can rest your elbows comfortably on its surface.

Tie a small knot at the free end of your pendulum string, and trail the knot and about an inch of the thread over the edge of the table.

Put your palms together, in the classic posture of praying hands. As you bring your hands together, trap the knot of your pendulum string between your right and left mounts of the Moon. Try it—you can do it far quicker than I can describe it.

Keeping the string secure between your palms, rest your elbows on the table, about 12 inches apart. The pendulum should hang down between your arms. If the weight touches the table, the string is too long. Cut it shorter, tie another knot near the free end, and repeat the setting up process.

Now you are ready to program your Moon connection pendulum. Close your eyes. Either aloud or in your mind, ask a question which has a definite yes answer. "Am I sitting at a table?" is fine. "Can a duck swim?" is also suitable.

The only feature of your question is that you must know that the answer is yes. About ten se-

Moon Techniques Quickly Bring Vast Profits

conds after making your inquiry, open your eyes. The pendulum will be swinging.

Note how it is swinging—side to side, to and fro, around in a circle, or in a figure eight. The shape of the swing will vary from person to person, but you will know that whenever your pendulum swings like that for you, it is answering "yes."

Lower your hands until the pendulum weight touches the table. Then, move your hands up again slowly, so that the weight clears the table. This movement is merely to stop the initial swing.

When the pendulum is more or less at rest, close your eyes and ask a question which you know has a negative answer. "Is this year 1975?" is an example. "Will a solid block of lead float on water?" is another query which will bring a firm "no" as an answer.

Open your eyes, and again note how the pendulum is swinging. It will be doing something differently from the way it was behaving the last time you opened your eyes.

Whatever path the weight is following, you will know that your pendulum is using that style of swing to tell you "no."

Following these simple preliminaries, you're all set to find something that is lost, or discover hidden treasure, by tapping into the mystic energies of the Moon connection.

If some personal possession is missing, ask your pendulum. A logical sequence of questions will zero you in on the location of the object.

Moon Techniques Quickly Bring Vast Profits

"Is it in the house?" Yes, "Upstairs?" No. "In the basement?" Yes. "Near the stairs?" No. "Near the washer?" Yes.

"Under the washer?" No. "In the washer?" No. "To the side of the washer?" Yes. "Left?" No. "In the dryer?" No. "Behind the dryer?" Yes. That is a typical sequence of questions which located a missing wedding band.

An amateur prospector with whom I am acquainted lays out a map of the area he plans to visit. He makes a mark at a likely spot on the map, and asks his pendulum if there is gold to be found at that spot.

If he gets a negative, he asks if there is gold to the west, to the east, to the north, or to the south. When he gets an affirmative direction, he asks if it is less than a mile from the spot he has marked. Then he narrows it down to half a mile or a quarter of a mile.

He then marks the spot identified by the pendulum and asks if it is correct. If he receives confirmation, he asks if the gold is within 12 inches of the surface. Another affirmative has him asking if it's free gold, as opposed to gold-bearing rock which requires mining.

In this way, he knows days beforehand exactly where to go to pan for gold. His new truck and trailer home have both been fully financed with his gold discoveries.

Missing persons can also be located. A close acquaintance of mine was desperately seeking his teenage daughter who had run away from home. I taught him to use the Moon contact pendulum and

Moon Techniques Quickly Bring Vast Profits

he located exactly which seat of a rock concert the child would be in that evening. We drove there, and father and daughter were reunited at the predicted place.

The Moon connection will also uncover "treasure" in other ways.

VcToria Comments: *Stock trading is a nice one to do with the pendulum. If you have the original book that was published in 1980, then on page 140 you can read a case study from a letter sent to Geof.*

DETECT PRIVATE SECRETS WITH MOON CONTACT

This technique is a specialized application of the Moon contact. You already know the precise technique for setting this up, as I described it to you a few pages back, and you learned how to find out what your rivals are plotting. The same instructions apply here, with this one addition.

With your right Saturn finger resting across the palm, slide the tip back until it contacts the plain of Uranus, bringing your knuckle up as your finger bends. Keep the rest of your fingers as stationary as possible. Then, slide the Saturn finger back to where it was, in contact with the left mount of Mars.

Continue to do this back-and-forth slide as you relax with your eyes closed. Think clearly of any person you know, and into your mind will flood facts about what that person is planning to do, and what will happen to him or her in coming days and weeks.

The earlier description of the Moon contact is a way to find out what people are doing at the time you perform the technique. This advanced version takes you a quantum leap ahead of that, giving you a view of the future, a massive advantage in any situation.

You can forecast the future of anyone, including yourself. How far can you see up the time path with this method? With precise accuracy, you can forecast about a week or ten days ahead. More generally, you can predict with reasonable precision for up to six months. In broad outline, you can pull in data from as far as five years into the future.

The reason for the reduction in exactness is an inevitable consequence of human life. Our future is not firm, fixed, and totally preordained.

Every human being has the God-given faculty of free will. We can change our minds about taking an action, and so change our ordained future at any time. Thus, the further ahead we peer into the mists of time, the more free will decisions can later come along to alter the precise forecast.

Nevertheless, the amount of accurate data you can realize in advance is incredibly useful in your path of seeking benefits.

The Moon contact thoughts or pictures that come to you as you move your finger up and down will be clear and precise. They will "feel" quite different from your usual mental processes, almost as if someone else were using your brain to do your thinking for you. As before, this is a difficult concept to express on paper, but once it has happened to you, and you've checked the facts later and proved the accuracy of your predictions, you'll know that this Moon contact does indeed bridge time and

Moon Techniques Quickly Bring Vast Profits

space, bringing you exactly the same kind of data used by top-flight psychics in their daily work.

There's no need for you to hang out a shingle saying "Psychic—Knows All, Tells All." Use the secrets unobtrusively.

VcToria Comments: *A good psychic will get word of mouth referrals.*

With this technique above, use it about thirty minutes before your client arrives. Picture how you think they might look if it is a first time client and all you have is their first name. This gives you good idea of the quality of the read that you will be doing from the moment they step through the door.

MOON TECHNIQUES ARE IRRESISTIBLE UNLESS YOU KNOW THIS SECRET

It can be somewhat frightening to think that anyone who owns this book can sneak unseen into your life and find out what you're doing, and what you're going to do.

I agree, and here's how to prevent that kind of trespassing from happening to you.

There's no need to erect this *Moon barrier* every hour of the day. As you get into the swing of using iso-bionic energy, you'll be able to tell when someone else is using similar techniques around you. The practice sets up a kind of mental watchdog in your mind, and anyone who tries to work Acupineology techniques to your detriment will be instantly recognized by you.

How will you find this out? Indescribably! Take it from me, you'll not only know who is tripping

Moon Techniques Quickly Bring Vast Profits

around you with iso-bionic energy, but you'll also know exactly what they're doing, and what they're expecting to gain from the routine.

You may decide to cooperate. The other Acupineologist may be helping to heal you of a malady or assist you in some other way. Acu-Key 9 suggests how you can be generous with your new-found powers.

But you may decide that you do not want the other person snooping around with iso-bionic energy. You may detect that although the results will benefit the other person, you'll be on the losing end.

So build this Moon barrier, and sail on your way untouched.

The moment you detect unwanted iso-bionic energy interference, place the tip of your right thumb in your left plain of Uranus, and touch the tip of your left Saturn finger to your right mount of Saturn.

That gesture at once erects an intangible wall which no other person can penetrate with natural energy techniques.

If you're alone, or not being observed by anyone, you can strengthen the barrier by holding your hands up in the described gesture, looking out through the space between your right thumb and your left Saturn finger, and turning around slowly to your right until you're facing the same way again.

You will at once feel the presence of anyone else's iso-bionic energy dwindle, fade, and withdraw. The Moon barrier remains in place for 28 days, or one complete set of moon phases, so you need to

Moon Techniques Quickly Bring Vast Profits

perform this routine only once a month to keep any prolonged attempt at psychic spying permanently at bay.

And now, onward to Acu-Key 6, where you will learn to take even more extensive and valuable trips into unseen dimensions of profit and peace.

VcToria Comments: *If you have either one of the two previously re-published books The Mystic Grimoire of Mighty Spells and Rituals by Frater Malak AKA Geof Gray-Cobb or NAP The Miracle of New Avatar Power by Geof Gray-Cobb then the back pages offer a monthly 'spell' with energy sent out to the group. You may apply this one technique at this time for your monthly protection.*

Specialized Moon Concepts for Taking Profitable Psychic Journeys

Your iso-bionic energy fields have a fascinating property which you can use to have truly "far out" experiences. Aside from impinging on everything around you, whether tangible or abstract, these lines of force have the ability to carry your intelligence, your awareness—the thinking, seeing, experiencing you—to any place you contemplate.

ASTRAL TRAVEL CUTS THE SURLY BONDS OF EARTH

If you have some knowledge of *astral travel*—also known as *astral projection* or *out-of-body experiences*—then the above paragraph is clear to you. By stimulating the appropriate lines of force, astral travel becomes an automatic process for you.

What exactly is astral travel? Researchers have so far been defeated in their efforts to find a precise explanation and description of it. My suggestion is that you experience it, and then you'll know what goes on when you travel astrally. You'll know with a personal certainty, which is clearer than any printed or verbal explanation could be.

An authentic astral journey starts and ends at your couch, bed, or chair. You sit or lie comfortably and close your eyes. To any outside observer who

Specialized Moon Concepts

sees you doing this, you will then seem to fall deeply asleep.

But, inside your head a very different panorama is unfolding. As you astrally project, you'll find yourself walking or floating away from your physical body. Your vital functions, such as heartbeat, breathing, digestion, and all the factors that keep your physical body mobile and alive, continue as they do when you slumber.

Your awareness of the world is the difference. You're in a very different space. Traveling along iso-bionic lines of force, you can go anywhere in the flick of an eye. With you go your five senses. You can see where you are, hear everything around you, smell, taste, and—to a greater or lesser degree—touch and feel material objects.

You can travel anywhere on earth: to your neighbor's house to wander around, invisible and undetectable; to far-flung cities and countries, to watch events unfold on the far side of the world; to stars and planets; to the depths of oceans—the entire universe is yours to explore when you're in the astral state.

Even more amazingly, you can slip astralward to the *astral plane*, where you will meet fellow astral travelers, and converse, enjoy, and communicate. The astral plane is only the threshold to even more inspirational planes of existence which defy description.

It would be better for you to live these ineffable happenings while you're astral tripping, rather than having me try to give pages of description. One trip

Specialized Moon Concepts

there and you'll have a clear picture of what I can only hint at.

GIANT STEPS TOWARD YOUR GOALS WITH THE ASTRAL VISITATION

Have I sketched the picture clearly enough? When you perform astral travel, your physical body—the one you weigh on the bathroom scale—sleeps soundly, while the real you, fully alert and awake, roams wherever you wish.

The fields of experience thus opened up are infinite in their benefits for you, at material, mental, or spiritual levels.

To reach the state of mind and body with which you can begin these thrilling travels, you need a comfortable place. Your attention is going to be away from your body for a while, and if it needs anything while you're "gone," you'll come flashing back at the speed of light, cutting short whatever stimulating episode you might have been enjoying with this special Moon concept.

So, before any astral journey, favor yourself a little. Visit the washroom. Be sure you are not starving—although you shouldn't be stuffed with food or drink either. The discomfort of either hunger or indigestion, are sure-fire signals from your body that bring you sharply back to the astral plane.

Try to ensure that the temperature is comfortable. Sweating with heat or shivering from the cold will erode your astral travel enjoyment.

In short, the bodily conditions for astral travel are very similar to those you need to get a good night's

Specialized Moon Concepts

sleep, or for nodding off in your favorite chair for a while.

However, you do have one advantage over the learning process of any other new skill. Although you may not be aware of it, you've been traveling astrally all your life. Many dreams are actually astral journeys, and what this Moon concept does is to give you full control over where you go and what you do, a feature which is lacking from most ordinary dreams.

The Moon concept also adds a feature to the experience which mars involuntary astral trips. You retain a full and complete memory of your experience.

Being able to recall your journey is probably the most important feature of authentic astral travel. Even in the material world, if you go somewhere and then forget every detail of what you did and saw, the experience is lost, and you might as well have never gone in the first place.

The same is true for astral travel. Almost certainly, you have traveled while you've been sleeping to an astral place known to many people as the *Astral City of New Psychic Power** But the memories of that place may be dim and indistinct.

VcToria Comments: *"The Astral City of New Psychic Power" is explained and explored more fully in the book "Secrets from Beyond the Pyramids" being republished and slightly re-edited and due for release in November 2019, also written by Geof Gray-Cobb.*

This Moon technique ensures that you will keep every nuance and factor clearly in your memory when you "come back."

Specialized Moon Concepts

Assuming that you have arranged your physical body comfortably, you're now ready to take an astral trip.

This is one Acupineology technique which takes time. In the astral plane, the clock often moves ahead at the same rate as the clock on your material wall, so if you spend an hour in the astral plane, when you return you'll find a full hour has elapsed in your room.

This is not necessarily true for all astral plane journeys. Many cases are on record in which people have had astral experiences which lasted for hours or days—in one well recorded case, years—and returned to the material world to find that only a few minutes had gone by.

The old saying alluding to having to walk before you can run applies admirably to astral travel. First, you should become familiar with the astral plane locally. Travel around your home, out into the surrounding streets, into buildings and places fairly close to your base. Later, you can embark on more ambitious trips.

Once you've physically set up the time and place, close your eyes. Place the mount of the Moon of your left hand in contact with your umbilical focus.

Place the mount of the Moon of your right hand on your pectoral focus.

Take five deep breaths and allow yourself to sink into relaxation. If you're sitting, your hands will fall to your lap. That's fine—it shows that you are relaxing. In fact, if you are seated and your hands do not slide down your chest and abdomen that shows

Specialized Moon Concepts

that you're still tense. A prerequisite for efficient astral travel is that you must be as limp and relaxed as a rag doll.

Now, let things happen by themselves. Drift with the waves of peace that wash over you, feeling very much the same as you do when you drop off to sleep. On no account should you try to force any change by an act of will.

At some stage in the drifting process, you'll realize that you've made it! You're free and clear of your physical body, which slumps quietly on your chair or couch.

Turn this first astral trip into an astral visitation. Think of any place not far away that you know well, such as another room in your home, your neighbor's living room, or the store on your block. Anywhere will do, but it must be a place with which you are familiar.

Zap! You're there. Look around you, listen to anything going on, and take an interest in whatever anyone is doing who is there at the time. You're invisible and intangible, so there's no need to worry about being discovered.

Keep the trip fairly brief, no matter how fascinating it may be to observe what your friends are doing in private. When you've absorbed a few minutes of the scene, think about the room from which you started the trip.

Once again, you will move in a flash. You'll be back there at once. Open your eyes, and recall where you have been, what you heard, and what was going on.

Specialized Moon Concepts

That's enough for a first time. Practice the technique whenever you have quiet moments. Set up for astral visitations as you settle down in bed at night, and take a brief astral journey before going to sleep.

VcToria Comments: *If you do decide to do this just prior to sleep know you may drift off to sleep. However, your dreams will be magnified, so do keep a journal and pen or some recording device beside your bed. I do not recommend a cell phone. The vibrations of these disturb the energy needed to sleep. I also recommend that you leave the cell phone off and in another room when practicing astral traveling.*

USE AKASHIC AWARENESS TO TALK TO MYSTIC BEINGS

Once you are familiar with the local astral plane, you can become even more ambitious. Try journeys to places you have never visited. You'll rapidly gain confidence in this life changing mode of free travel.

As your trips expand, you'll begin meeting other people who are also traveling astrally. Your encounters will be as real and meaningful as any you enjoy in the material world.

Eventually, most likely after you have visited the Astral City I mentioned earlier, you will become aware that you can take a step into other dimensions, which defy verbal description. When you return from such a journey, you'll have had experiences that are impossible to write down. Energy fields, love, centers of intelligence, light,

Specialized Moon Concepts

protection, and peacefulness are some of the abstractions you will encounter.

In such dimensions, you will begin to acquire *akashic awareness*, which is knowledge of how the universe operates, your place in it, and the whole awesome picture of the harmony built by your Creator into this miraculous place in which we live and breathe.

After some thrilling time, you'll return from your astral journey knowing that you've met and talked with a Master, a mystic being who has your welfare at heart and has given you wise words of guidance and love.

Whom will you meet? Names are only labels. Your Guardian Angel, one of the Lords of Flame, an Avatar, a Seraph . . . these are merely titles we give to the unseen protectors you may encounter. You will know the purpose of the being you meet, even if you do not bring back a calling card with a name, title, address, and telephone number on it!

Please understand that I am purposely sketching the delights of astral travel in outline only. You will travel more satisfactorily and profitably if you have few preconceived notions about the astral and other planes.

I agree that much of this section probably seems very mystical and airy-fairy, apparently unconnected with paying bills, buying food, and keeping your body and soul comfortably together. Believe me when I tell you that the struggles at the material level will become easier as you penetrate more deeply into the abstract levels, and find guidance flowing toward you.

Specialized Moon Concepts

HAVE YOU LIVED BEFORE?

Do you believe in reincarnation? If you do, you're aligned with many religious teachers whose beliefs and faiths have been around for thousands of years.

Simply stated, the theory of reincarnation suggests that your soul, the ball of energy which is the individual "you," exists for eternity. During the soul's journey toward unfathomable rewards, part of the time is spent inhabiting physical bodies here on earth.

Your soul enters the growing fetus of an unborn child, is born with the baby, and grows to adulthood. Eventually, the physical body wears out and the soul passes on, leaving that body.

After a period of time, the soul is born in another human body, years or centuries later, and lives another life, gathering new experiences until death once again separates the body and the soul.

Some religions see this happening hundreds of times during the soul's journey. Other mystical teachings theorize that we undergo relatively few reincarnations.

Naturally, as with any theory which has yet to be proven to everyone's satisfaction, some people deny the possibility of reincarnation altogether, suggesting that we are born but once on earth, and when we die we never return to this vale of tears.

Discover your reincarnation path

Acupineology enables you to investigate the theory of reincarnation and reach your own conclusions. On the way to your decision, you can pick up startling evidence, much of which you can use for your greater benefit.

Some young children can sit down at the piano and compose symphonies, others can paint pictures, write poetry, or handle higher math when their pals are still struggling with one-and-one-makes-two. The simplest explanation for the wonders of child prodigies is to suggest that they may have been composers, artists, poets, or scientists in a previous life, and have somehow brought their knowledge back with them.

You may not have been a famous person in your earlier lives, but while you're making up your mind about reincarnation, you may discover that you possess unknown skills which can only be explained by your having mastered them in some other time and existence.

These resurrected skills can have distinct marketable value in this life. That's what I mean when I say that you may pick up evidence to use for material gain.

Travel to other times and places

This Moon technique is a variation on the astral travel method described earlier. It will help your reincarnation research enormously if you have already mastered astral travel before dipping further into these mysteries of time and space.

Your first journeys into the akashic levels, where evidence of your previous lives can exist, are best carried out when you are sleeping. The concept of reincarnation might seem to be at odds with the learned logic of your conscious mind, so you will need to suspend your disbelief. What better way to allow your inner mind free rein than when you're sound asleep?

As you finally settle down toward slumber, and when you've switched off the late show and extinguished the light, arrange your mounts of the Moon as instructed for starting astral travel.

Take five deep breaths. Then, in your mind, begin counting backward from 100 down to 1. Make this a slow count, with a distinct pause between each number.

If you are still aware that you're in bed when you reach 1, arrange yourself for sleep in your usual posture, and let it come naturally as you normally drop into the arms of Morpheus. You've primed your mind, and iso-bionic energy wheels are turning at astral and akashic levels.

Next morning, review any dreams you have had. Were you in another period of time, another city, another body (male or female), another country?

If you have dreamed anything out of character with your regular existence, make a note of it. This can be the start of total reincarnation recall.

During the day, pay attention to yourself. Does that sound strange? Most of the time, we let our bodies and our minds do their own things, especially if we're caught up with routine jobs, or walking, driving, or being driven in familiar surroundings.

The mind stimulation of the Moon contact can bring new and interesting ideas flickering through your mind. That's why I suggest that you pay attention to yourself. Maybe you'll think about pursuing a hobby you've never tried. Perhaps you

Specialized Moon Concepts

will decide to plan for a trip to new horizons. A thousand and one unusual impressions can give you clues to the levels of mind you have been stimulating.

Another life?

Continue with the reincarnation search on any night when you're not busy with other Acupineology techniques. As you proceed with the process, be alert for signs that you're getting down to a mother lode of experience which you certainly have not had during this life so far.

Somewhere along the line, you'll find a name. It will be your name, but not the name you're using right now. It will be a name which fits you like a glove, even though you may never recall having heard it before.

Details will begin to click into place. A trade may show up in your research. If feasible, spend a weekend checking on whether you've retained any skills from this theoretical previous life.

One morning, you'll awaken to find that you've achieved a breakthrough. You'll have uncovered a whole chunk of your earlier existence. You'll know your wife's name, what you did, where you lived, and specific details of the life of someone who may have lived in ancient Egypt, mystic Tibet, medieval Germany, or similar places now remote from you in time and space.

You may find this to be an absorbing field of true psychic research, and most definitely keyed to the here and now so far as mundane benefits are concerned.

PREVIOUS INCARNATION KNOWLEDGE CAN MEAN MONEY IN THE BANK

"But there's no proof that the things I find out are true," you may say. "I've put together a clear narrative of me as a temple maiden to one of the old Mayan priests, but there's no hope of ever proving it to anyone else."

You're right. Only you, in the security of your knowledge, because you've lived the life, can be certain that you've existed before. Nevertheless, the knowledge is neither academic nor useless.

As you develop the picture, you'll also begin to acquire the aptitudes of your previous life. It's a rare past life that does not reveal a talent which can be turned to a profit.

Even if you should find a life where abilities and skills have no relevance to modern life, go looking for another life. If you've had one bout of reincarnation, you've almost certainly had others.

Probe a little deeper into this concept. I'm not simply referring to marketable skills, like carpentry, doctoring, mathematical ability, or chariot racing. (Yes, I know a jockey who has his own undeniable evidence that he raced chariots in ancient Rome!)

Besides manual or mental job skills, your past lives will contain attitudes and outlooks which are directly useful in making your life more harmonious.

In many cases, the succession of lives of a soul seems to swing like a pendulum. For example, a person who was a helpless invalid in one life may become a virile and helpful surgeon in the next life.

Specialized Moon Concepts

A savage warrior may spend his succeeding life as a mediator in labor disputes, keeping the peace as diligently as he made war during the previous life.

So, as you accumulate reincarnation data, look for factors which are opposed to your present conditions and these might help you.

If you're uptight much of the time, living on frazzled nerves, you are likely to find a previous life where you were a serene religious leader who could be fazed by nothing or no one. Bring some of that peace of mind into this present life and you'll know how to handle it, because in your research you'll have experienced being that calm and peaceful person.

Perhaps you're always being put down, because you're too easygoing. In a past life, you'll probably find a time when you were a real martinet of a boss. Absorb some of that aggressiveness, and use it the next time someone tries to impose on you.

Moon contacts in search of previous lives open infinite horizons to reach harmony and progress. Give the technique a try. It surely beats dropping off to sleep and just snoring eight hours!

DREAM GUIDING AND MIND TOUCHING: TWIN HIGHROADS TO THE TOP

While practicing astral travel and reincarnation investigation, you will acquire a number of associated abilities that require only a minor honing to put you miles ahead of the pack.

Specialized Moon Concepts

Dream guiding and *mind touching* are really extensions of astral travel, and I've labeled them merely for convenience of definition.

Dream guiding

Dream guiding is the sharp and incisive extension to astral travel that lets you influence anything going on anywhere in the material world, and to turn events in your favor.

As you persevere with astral travel techniques, your mind will automatically become a powerful instrument. On nights when you decide to take a normal night's sleep, you can have fun with your ordinary dreams. You'll find you can shape and steer those dreams into any shape or situation you wish.

Having run through a kind of dream rehearsal of an event, you'll often find the situation you created in the sleep state happening in real life, with you in command as firmly as you were in the dream.

Once you have the smallest amount of success with astral travel, try dream guiding the next time you realize you're dreaming. The process is as simple to state as it is easy to do: Think it, and it will happen.

As you progress, you'll become an expert at this ability to stand to one side and watch what's happening in your dreams, and then, like a movie director, you can change the course of the unfolding drama. And naturally, you'll alter it so that you come out on top!

No matter what you hanker after, dream guiding will help you toward your goal.

Specialized Moon Concepts

If you're looking for a loving partner, grab hold of the next dream that comes along, and dream guide exactly the right person to walk into that dream, responding to you, obeying you, cohabiting with you, and behaving exactly as you would desire in the waking state.

Then, be prepared to be amazed as the coming days and weeks bring that dream relationship into genuine reality.

This is an authentic way of literally making your dreams come true. You set the stage in the sleep state, and the iso-bionic energy you've created during your regular Acupineology workouts will do the rest.

Mind touching

Have you ever had an impulse to do something, and afterward wondered, "Why did I do that?"

It could be that someone around you knows the technique of mind touching. Master this simple technique, and you can also have the world obeying your slightest whim, without knowing why.

Mind touching is exactly what the name implies. You mentally move in on the mind of anyone you wish and plant an idea which the person will act upon later.

Hundreds of opportunities exist for you to gain advantages with this technique. You can impel a loan officer to grant you an astounding amount at conditions which fit your situation. You can have your enemy literally crawl to your door to apologize for behaving so terribly.

Specialized Moon Concepts

Certain personal habits of your associates can be changed so that they no longer bug you. Without cheating or breaking the rules, you can be sure to come out ahead of rivals in any kind of competition, by convincing them that they're going to end up behind you.

Mind touching is a technique that can bring what you want from people without any browbeating, hypnosis, aggression, or hard physical labor.

Mind touching is carried out when the person you wish to influence is sleeping. That might require some juggling of schedules on your part, so that you'll be awake when your target is asleep.

The hours of darkness are when most people sleep, so try your first attempts at mind touching late in the evening.

Set yourself up for astral travel and move into the astral state. Think yourself into the sleeping quarters of the person you wish to influence. If the bed is empty, or your target is still watching TV, reading, or making love, move out and try again some other time.

Eventually, you will make contact with your target when he or she is sleeping. Your target may be unconsciously astrally traveling himself. If so, you may see a silver cord of energy wreathing out of the slumbering body, connecting at the other end with the person's astral presence. If you see the silver cord, that's excellent. It means that the target is deeply unconscious of your presence.

Stand beside the bed and reach out your astral hands to touch your fingers to the brow of the

Specialized Moon Concepts

sleeper. Be careful, now. In the astral state, your presence is so refined that you can drift through solid objects like a hot knife through butter. Be sure to stop your hands before they penetrate the sleeper's skull. It doesn't matter if they do move inside the skull, but being up to your wrists in someone's head can be something of a shock to a fledgling astral traveler.

Now, with your mind in the astral state as you stand there, pronounce what you wish the sleeper to do for you in his or her waking hours.

"You will reverse your refusal of a loan and instead grant me the money I need."

"You will call me and apologize abjectly for your negative attitudes."

"You will promote me, and give me a fat raise."

"You will stop pressing your repulsive attentions on me."

"You will be unable to be fully efficient when we compete and you already know I shall win."

These are typical statements that you can impress upon the mind of a sleeper. Having performed the mind touching, go on your way, rejoicing, to other astral adventures.

Then, watch your statement become reality in the waking state, as your target unwittingly follows your astrally planted instructions.

Specialized Moon Concepts

SAFETY FROM MIND INTRUSION WITH THIS MOON DEFENSE

The technique of mind touching is neither copyrighted nor particularly secret. It is merely my name for a recognized occult discipline for influencing other people without their knowledge.

As a safety precaution, this Moon defense takes mere seconds to perform, and ensures that you will not be unconsciously influenced by anyone who knows and uses the techniques described above.

Put your two palms together in the attitudes of prayer I described earlier, and separate all of your fingers except your Saturn fingers. Hold them together as you think the words, "Outer darkness, inner light."

This gesture, used with the Moon barrier, makes an impenetrable energy screen, protecting you from all astral interference.

Just possibly, you may come across someone who knows these defenses when you are attempting mind touching. You'll recognize the defense. The slumbering body will be resting inside an egg-shaped container of visible, blue-white energy.

If that proves to be the case, you'll have to use some method other than mind touching. With that energy barrier erected, you won't be able to get near your sleeping target. His Moon defense has wrapped him in a shield which is as impervious to you as bulletproof glass.

The positive angle of such a disappointment is that you'll see, firsthand, the total efficiency of the

Specialized Moon Concepts

barrier you yourself are putting up each sleeping period with the Moon defense.

Once it is erected, the Moon defense remains powerful for a minimum of 24 hours.

Onward, friend. In Acu-Key 7, which follows next, you're going to add even more power to your already strong energy fields.

Additional Shattering Strength from Alpha-Numeric Tones

If you stand close to a piano, depress the sustaining pedal, and sing a note loudly, you'll find that when you stop, the piano will still be "singing" your note quietly. A guitar will do the same thing if you sing the note of one of the strings. After the sound of your voice ceases, the guitar will continue to hum the note.

That phenomenon is known as *sympathetic resonance* or *vibration*, and it forms part of a technique which builds your iso-bionic energy efforts to irresistible peaks.

AS ABOVE, SO BELOW

Whether we look at the cycles of planets around the sun, the swings of a pendulum, the vibrations of a violin string, or the orbits of electrons in an atom, we see that our world is made up of vibrations of varying speeds and wavelengths. Your work with iso-bionic energy relies on that fact, combined with the ancient occult wisdom summarized by Hermes Trismegistus, who said, "That which is above, is as that which is below."

That brief phrase sums up this whole universe. Somewhere in the astral or adjacent planes is what you lack, and by making the right vibration, sympathetic resonance brings it into being in the material world.

If that concept takes a little digesting, disregard it for the moment, and let us proceed to the practical application of the thought. Suffice it to say that the vibrations of iso-bionic energy will, as promised, bring you anything you need, and all you have to do is be in the right place to receive and enjoy the bounty.

Your Acupineology practice will open up channels for the vibrations of the cosmos, and your requests will be granted. They have to be, because you are in tune with the natural energies which created you and everything around you.

THE RIGHT SOUND REELS IN YOUR WISH

So, how do you go about making the creative planes vibrate in sympathy with your needs?

You have already started that magic process, with your psinic vibration, pectoral swell, and umbilical resonance, which you'll be practicing on a daily basis.

I will now offer you a variation in the ways of making these sounds, increasing their power by a quantum leap. When you add these modifications, the appropriate lines of force will reach out into the unseen planes, vibrate the correct creative sphere, and, through the mysterious workings of fate and destiny, "that which was above will now be below." This means that your mental desire will turn miraculously into a material object, or "real" condition.

Alpha-Numeric Tones

You may want to refresh your memory on how to create the basic psinic, pectoral, and umbilical sounds. The instructions for them are in Acu-Key 1, starting on page 25.

Do not be concerned about referring back and forth in this book. You're absorbing a great deal of data, and I would not expect you to hold it all in your mind after one reading.

In the final section of this book, Acu-Key 9, we will knit all of this instructional material together into one logical parcel, tailored specifically to allow the vibrations of the universe to create your special and individual destiny.

THE ALPHA-TONES FOR YOUR PSINIC VIBRATION

You may recall from Acu-Key 1 that you create your psinic vibration by making the sound of the letter "E," keeping it vibrating for a while, and then repeating it twice.

In the final section of this Acu-Key, you're going to discover how to add the magic of *numerology* to your personal life style program, and by adding *alpha-tones* to your psinic vibration, you will impose a letter and a number on the tone, and thus resonate your psinic field to that number and letter.

All of the alpha-tones, as you might anticipate from the name, are composed of letters of the alphabet. The alpha-tones are: B, C, D, E, G, P, T, V, and Z.

You will notice that they all have the basic "E" sound which you used to create your psinic

Alpha-Numeric Tones

vibration. If you are British or Canadian, you may have been taught that the last letter of the alphabet is pronounced "zed." For the purpose of this iso-bionic exercise, please use the American name of the letter, which is "zee."

Superimposing an alpha-tone on your psinic vibration is simple. In place of the simple "E" sound you create three times, you should substitute one of the alpha-tone letters instead. A further modification is that you should now keep your lips open, so that the final "Eeeeeee" comes out of your mouth, not your nose as you were originally instructed.

Why the change? Because at the outset you need to get your psinic vibration going in your head, and closing your mouth forces the sound to go through your nasal cavities. Practice your psinic vibration so that, even though you leave your mouth open, the sound still vibrates more in your head than in your throat and chest.

Each alpha-tone is connected with a number. Which number to use, and when to use it, is clearly explained in your personal program of Acupineology.

The numbers run from 1 through 9, and later I'll be telling you which numbers go with which letters.

THE BETA-TONES FOR YOUR PECTORAL SWELL

Having explained how to apply alpha-tones to your psinic vibration, we're off and running toward the application of *beta- tones* to your pectoral swell.

Alpha-Numeric Tones

As before, you impose a letter on the sound you are creating, bringing the power of numerology to bear on your pectoral field.

The beta-tones are the letters A, J, K, O, Q, R, U, and W. The procedure for superimposing a beta-tone on your pectoral swell is much the same as the modification to your psinic vibration which I explained to you earlier.

In place of the simple "A" sound you make when producing your pectoral swell, you substitute a beta-tone letter. I've instructed you on how the pectoral swell feels in your chest. You merely change the sound from "A" to one of the beta-tones.

I'm aware that "W" has three syllables. You will be told how to incorporate that letter shortly.

THE SIGMA-TONES
FOR YOUR UMBILICAL RESONANCE

Since I have already explained how to modify both your psinic vibration and pectoral swell, this explanation of the *sigma-tones* for your umbilical resonance will be relatively brief.

The sigma-tones, which go along with your resonance, are F, H, I, L, M, N, S, X, and Y. Instead of starting with the letter "M" as you were instructed in Acu-Key 1, experiment with turning the names of the sigma-tone letters into the same kind of breathy, internal rumble which makes a good umbilical resonance.

This might take some practice, and you may have to return to square one, starting with a whisper as I previously advised you, and gradually

Alpha-Numeric Tones

amplifying it into the powerful energy-stimulating sound which makes up the umbilical resonance.

NOW ADD THE MAGIC OF NUMEROLOGY

As I explained to you, each of your alpha-, beta- and sigma-tones vibrates to a number from 1 through 9. You will now learn how to put the correct number vibration into your Acupineology work whenever you are creating a personal life change routine.

Each day of the year carries a numerological vibration, based on the calendar date. All numbers can be reduced by numerology to a single number, and calendar dates, being numbers, are no exception.

Whenever you are doing an Acupineology routine which uses any of the tones, you should write down the date, to discover the day's basic vibration number.

Year vibration number

Write out the number of the year in full. Add the numbers you have written together. If your total is 10 or higher, add those numbers together, until you have a single figure from 1 to 9.

Example: If the year is 2019, you add together 2 plus 0 plus 1 plus 9, making a total of 12. Add those two numbers: 1 plus 2 equals 3.

The year 2019, therefore, carries the vibration of 3, a number related to creativity. Make a note of the year vibration number.

Alpha-Numeric Tones

Month vibration number

Now you need to discover the vibration number for the month. That's simple, because we already allocate numbers to months when we abbreviate the date. January is 1, February is 2, and so on, up to December, which is 12.

So, the first nine months of the year, up to and including September, are already numbered with a single number, which is what we need.

The final three months of the year need their identity numbers reduced to a single digit, just as we did with the number of the year.

October, the tenth month, vibrates to 10, which you total: 1 plus zero equals 1. October, like January, is a 1 month.

November, eleventh on the calendar, totals to 2. Lastly, December, the twelfth month, adds up to 3.

You made a note of the year vibration. Now write the month vibration number beside it.

Day vibration number

The next step is to reduce the date number to a single digit, if necessary. You use the same procedure. If the day you're working is a double-digit date, add the figures together, until you reach a number from 1 through 9.

If it's the 14th of the month, you add 1 and 4, producing 5. If it happens to be the 26th, you add 2 and 6, making 8. A few dates will need adding twice: the 29th totals to 11, so 11 is again totaled, and you end up with the knowledge that the 29th vibrates to the number 2.

Alpha-Numeric Tones

Write down the vibration number of the day alongside the year vibration number and the month vibration number.

Total all three. If you reach a double-digit total, add them together again. Eventually, you'll reach a single digit, and that's the final number you've been aiming to reach.

Complete example: Let's say today is June 27th 2019. Your year vibration number is 3. You reached that by adding 2 plus 0 plus 1 plus 9, which is 12. Then, 1 plus 2 is 3. The month vibration number is 6, June being the sixth month of the year. The 27th vibrates to 9, found by adding 2 and 7.

So, you've written down 3, 6, and 9. Add those together and you get 18. Add again, and the final digit is 9. So the vibration for any Acupineology work carried out by you on June 27th, 2019, should be keyed to the number 9. That took a while to explain, but it's truly simpler than it looks. Try a couple of examples on some scrap paper; you'll soon get into the swing of it.

THE RIGHT TONE FOR THE RIGHT DAY

Once you've found the vibration number for the day on which you're working with Acupineology, you can decide which of the tones to use for maximum effect when you're charging up your psinic, pectoral, and umbilical fields.

Alpha-tone numbers

The alpha-tone letters each have their individual numbers, and in a couple of cases we

Alpha-Numeric Tones

combine two letters to create a number that we need.

The number 1 is imposed on your psinic vibration by making the sound with the letter G, Pronounce it as a "soft" G, just as you might say, "Gee whiz!"

The number 2 is B or T, whichever you prefer. Number 3 is C; number 4 is D or V; number 5 is E.

The number 6 is made up of two letters: D and B. You start your vibration with "Deeeeee," and about halfway through the intonation, you say "B" and maintain the "Eeeeeee" sound to the end of the intonation. Repeat twice more as instructed.

The number 7 is P or G. If you choose to use G, it must be pronounced as a "hard" G, the way you say "geese" or "gear."

The number 8 is Z (pronounced "Zee," you recall), and number 9 is another double letter: P and T, used as I explained for number 6.

Beta-tone numbers

If you have read and understood the alpha-tone numbers above, I need only enumerate the letters and corresponding numbers for your beta-tones.

Number 1 is A or J; number 2 is K; number 3 is U; number 4 is U and A; number 5 is W; number 6 is O; number 7 is O and J; number 8 is Q; and number 9 is R.

In each case, you say the name, not the sound, of the letter. For instance, number 3 is "You," not "Uh!" and number 9 is "Are," not "Rerrrr!"

Alpha-Numeric Tones

The only one which is different from any which have gone before is number 5. Give the three syllables their full value, and spread them equally through each intonation: "Duh-bull-you," or—if this is the pronunciation you have been taught—"Duh-buh-you."

Sigma-tone numbers

These umbilical resonance sounds need to have little extra said about them. Number 1 is S; number 2 is T, but in this case you do not say the name of the letter. You use the sound, like "Tuh!" Think of it as if you were saying the word "Touch," without making the final "Ch" sound.

Number 3 is L; number 4 is M; number 5 is N; number 6 is F or X; number 7 is Y; number 8 is H; and number 9 is I (pronounced "Eye," of course).

INCREDIBLE ENERGY IS YOURS TO COMMAND

Adding the numerology vibrations of the date to your Acupineology work is probably the most powerful action you could add to the already super-energetic fields which will fulfill your smallest wish.

Notice that although you have been handed many different, interlocking techniques, I have yet to put the jigsaw together to make a complete picture for you.

This has been done purposely. I truly want you to know Acupineology from A to Z, before you create your overall miracle-working program. Hang in with me to the final section. You'll be glad you did!

Help Yourself to Miracles by Using Surplus Energy from Other People

Using iso-bionic energy with the techniques of Acupineology is a delightful give-and-take situation. You *take* the powers of the natural energies around you, and they *give* you whatever you ask for.

Other important features of iso-bionic energy relate to you and your fellow human beings. As you will discover, you can pass on your bounty to other people, to their eternal gratitude and admiration of you. Also, whenever you are below par with your energy levels, you can "top up" your iso-bionic batteries by taking a free ride on someone else's spare iso-bionic energy.

ISO-BIONIC ENERGY EBBS AND FLOWS

The preceding concept is extremely useful. Like the tides of the ocean, your iso-bionic energy, although it is always present and available, hits highs and lows. These up and down swings often coincide with the phases of the moon, as we might anticipate, since not only the sea, but also the air we breathe and the ground we walk on, are affected by the moon's gravitational pull.

Not everyone's energies hit their peaks at the same time. The science of *biorhythms* has investigated that phenomenon, and has found the energy

Using Surplus Energy From Other People

levels to correspond with the number of days that have passed since you were born.

So, whenever your iso-bionic energy is temporarily at slack tide, anyone you meet or contact is likely to have a stronger flow of iso-bionic energy than you have at that time.

In this Acu-Key, you will discover how to take splendid advantage of that factor. Your *iso-bionic tideway* opens you up to anyone's surplus energy and makes sure that your personal fields can sparkle to high miracle-working levels.

YOUR ISO-BIONIC TIDEWAY

If two pools of water are connected by a trench or conduit, the water will flow from the one with the higher water level until both pools are at the same level.

Your *iso-bionic tideway* works in a similar manner. You open up an energy channel between you and any person you choose, and if that person has a surplus of iso-bionic energy, you promptly find it coursing into your aura, charging you up and building the strength of your own iso-bionic energy fields.

The added benefit of this technique is that you never unwittingly allow an outflow of energy that you may need yourself. Your iso-bionic tideway has, in effect, a one-way valve which lets energy flow to you, but prevents energy from draining away from you—unless you wish that to happen.

Your left hand contains the iso-bionic energy points through which extra energy will be

Using Surplus Energy From Other People

automatically absorbed. These points are the tips of your Jupiter and Saturn finger (forefinger and second finger), or the mounts of those two planets.

When you bring these two fingers or mounts in contact with another person, your iso-bionic energies will receive a boost of any energy the other person has to spare.

Unless you're into massage or some other vocation which enables you to naturally lay your hands and fingers on other people, you can face a challenge in making contact with your iso-bionic tideway technique.

Fortunately, physical contact is not necessary. Iso-bionic energy easily spans empty space. It merely requires your mental intention and direction to draw a cascading stream of energy toward you, without having to lay hands on anyone's body.

This is the *tideway gesture* you need. Keeping your left Jupiter and Saturn fingers as straight as possible, curl your Sun and Mercury fingers into the palm of your hand, to make contact with the mount of Venus. Your thumb lies naturally alongside your Jupiter finger.

You now have your fingers of health and communication connected with the mount of attraction, while your stability and abundance fingers project like twin antennas, supported by your thumb, which helps with the rebuilding of your energy levels.

I have purposely used Acupineology terms in the preceding paragraph, so that you can get some idea of the theory behind this science. If the foregoing puzzles you, consult Figures 1 and 2 in

Using Surplus Energy From Other People

Acu-Key 1, and you'll understand the energy shape you have created with this gesture.

VcToria Comments: *If you bought this book directly from me you will have had an e-mail sent to you enabling you to print out the hand diagram so consult this.*

WHEN TO USE YOUR TIDEWAY GESTURE

As you move into the regular swing of your daily iso-bionic energy routines, you'll get to know the times when your energy fields are at peak power, and the times when, though adequate, they're not quite as vigorous.

Peak periods give you a tingling, bubbling feeling of well-being, and a quiet, certain knowledge that whatever you're setting out to do with iso-bionic energy will assuredly occur exactly the way you wish.

Lower levels of energy, while invigorating your mind and body, seem to lack that final "something" that confirms an overflowing abundance of this life-steering power.

The written word, as with a great deal of the description of iso-bionic energy's more abstract properties, is a blunt tool to try to get this concept across to you. It's safe to say that when you've been doing your iso-bionic energy routines for about four weeks, you'll feel the difference between highs and lows.

The days when you know your iso-bionic energy fields could use a boost are when you employ your tideway gesture. The gesture works unerringly, no

Using Surplus Energy From Other People

matter where you are or what you're doing, and you have many sources to pull that extra energy into your body and soul.

The bottom line suggestion is: *be unobtrusive.* This gesture needs no flourishes, arm waving, or attention attracting business. The finger positions open up an esoteric vacuum around you, and spare energy is literally sucked into your being.

Even making the gesture while you are reading this page will start the vital flow, but in practice, the closer you are to other people (within reason), the more energy you will absorb from their auras.

So, make the gesture secretly as you push your shopping cart around in a store. You can rest your left hand on the push bar of the cart in the tideway gesture and no one will be any wiser.

When traveling, it's easy to make the gesture under a coat thrown over your lap, or concealed by a purse or lunchbox. Out in the street, your left hand can make the gesture while it is in your pocket. At the movies, it's dark enough for you to casually make the gesture on your knee.

Try to arrange your Jupiter and Saturn fingers to point at someone. That's not absolutely necessary, but it helps. It doesn't matter if there is anything between you and the target. Your tideway gesture will efficiently bring you extra energy even if you are separated from someone else by a window, the back of a seat, or some other barrier.

Hold the gesture for no longer than it takes to make a slow count to 60, and then stop for at least two minutes to allow the new energy to be absorbed. Shorter periods will also be beneficial. Each time you

Using Surplus Energy From Other People

connect and aim the iso-bionic energy points, you receive a burst of energy from any iso-bionic fields around you.

While making the gesture, breathe a little more deeply than usual but not so enthusiastically that you hyperventilate and get dizzy.

As you carry out the tideway gesture, you will literally feel your iso-bionic energy fields charging up, making tingling sensations in various parts of your body. The tingle often occurs in your fingers, sometimes in your abdomen, or even the soles of your feet. This depends on which of your iso-bionic energy fields are receiving the booster shot.

VcToria Comments: *This is just my opinion on my Dad's work for this iso-bionic gesture ONLY. Be careful who you decide to relieve of energy whilst doing this gesture. You do not want to absorb negative energy. Being around happy children will always give you the proper boost and will not harm the child.*

ADD THESE TECHNIQUES TO YOUR TIDEWAY GESTURE FOR EVEN MORE EXTRAORDINARY RESULTS

When you're in the physical presence of anyone, you can take advantage of the situation by these applications of your tideway gesture.

You will chiefly gain extra power for your psinic field, helping you to become mentally as sharp as a new tack. Once that field is fully topped up, the overflow will augment your pectoral and umbilical fields, in that order.

Using Surplus Energy From Other People

This technique works well with social, business, or casual contacts during your waking hours. It is especially effective during meetings with neighbors, maybe over coffee; at lectures or in church, where you can draw iso-bionic energy from the speaker or minister; and in any other situation where a person is facing you so that you can see his or her forehead.

Make the tideway gesture casually, under the table, in your lap, even up against your left jaw as you rest your elbow. Any way will do, as long as you're not making a production out of it and attracting attention.

Arrange your Jupiter and Saturn fingers to point in the general direction of the person from whom you are going to draw extra energy. There's no need to sight the fingers like you would aim a handgun. Your target's maximum strength iso-bionic fields extend more than three feet around his or her body, and even further in lesser degrees.

Now focus your gaze on the middle of your target's brow, an inch or so above the bridge of the nose. That's the psinic focus, where the energy field comes to a surging peak of potential. By making this straight line connection with your eyes, you considerably reinforce the tideway gesture. The same slow count of 60 is long enough for one application, with a rest period of about two minutes if you're going to repeat the process.

Practicing this technique throughout a period of about a half-hour will bring you the familiar tingling sensations, and the certain knowledge that destiny is making your desires come gloriously true.

Using Surplus Energy From Other People

HOW TO DRAW ISO-BIONIC ENERGY FROM A SOCIAL HANDSHAKE

Instant energy charges are yours for the taking when anyone shakes you by the hand, as happens frequently to most of us during our day-to-day lives. Whether it's an acquaintance or a politician stumping your neighborhood, you should be alert for this super-powerful booster method.

As the person who is greeting you, or being introduced, extends his or her hand, look down and connect your gaze with the tip of his thumb.

At once sweep your eyes upward or across to your target's umbilical focus, on up to the pectoral focus, and end up by looking at his psinic focus.

This takes only a second or two, and is a perfectly normal eye movement. Try to time the sweep of your eyes so that, as your hands touch, you have just started to look at the psinic focus in your target's brow.

Make a normal handshake, adding just a hint more pressure to your Jupiter and Saturn fingers to make firm contact. There's no need to prolong the physical contact, or shake the person's arm off. At the moment of contact, an invisible spark of iso-bionic energy will flash from the other person's fields into your own.

Break both your eye contact with the psinic focus and your grip simultaneously, and conduct yourself normally thereafter, even if your hands and limbs are tingling to the thrill of this energy surge.

Sometimes the exchange can be so powerful that your target will actually feel his or her energy

Using Surplus Energy From Other People

level fall. We can find an example of this in the Bible, where Jesus's garment was touched by a woman in the crowd.

Jesus at once asked who had touched him, "for he knew that virtue had gone out of him."* Using our present-day terms, that corresponds to the woman absorbing a charge of iso-bionic energy from Jesus. You may recall that she was instantly healed.

That's the kind of energy surge you set up with a handshake like the one described above. Male, female, old, or young, this contact soaks iso-bionic energy into you like dry summer soil welcoming a rainfall.

*Mark, 5:30.

WHAT COMES NEXT?

Congratulations on staying with me thus far. You have now been given the most powerful method I currently know to change your life.

We're not quite through yet. You have the method, but you have yet to learn exactly where and when to apply it. That follows in Acu-Key 9, where you will put it all together in a glittering, joyful schedule of life-improvement.

So far, I have shown you the techniques and illustrated many with typical case histories.

VcToria Comments: *I have removed all the case history claims to bring the book into an instructional only version. Many folks asked for the books to be re-published and have these stories removed. If you wish to buy a copy of the original book you may now*

Using Surplus Energy From Other People

do so at a much better cost. By re-publishing this book the older ones are no longer 'rare'.

I have generally steered around the theory about why iso-bionic energy works so well, partly because research is still in the process of providing precise answers, but more cogently because I'm oriented more toward results and consequences that you can savor, than toward explanations of why these results occur.

I'm what's known as a pragmatist. If it works and brings joy, harmony, and freedom from pain and frustration, go with it. Explanations and theories can come later.

I know you'll be prompted to write to me and tell me of your towering successes. I thank you sincerely in advance, and this printed gratitude may be my only way of expressing my appreciation for your time, effort, and the cost of stamp and paper. I truly enjoy receiving letters sent on to me by my publisher, but I get such piles of mail, I can personally reply to a mere fraction of them. So if you do write, be assured that I've enjoyed your letter, and that I have possibly filed it away to use as a case history or example of a technique in some future book.

VcToria Comments: *I left my Dad's 'thank you' paragraph in as I am sure you, the reader, know that he is passed over to the other side. [May 12th 2009] Having informed you of this you may e-mail me with any stories that you wish to share. Please let me know if you would like them printed in further books to be written. I need your written permission to copy them.*

Using Surplus Energy From Other People

YOUR ACUPINEOLOGY PROGRAM BRINGS RICHES AT ALL LEVELS OF BEING

Throughout the preceding pages, I have deliberately handed you many portions of information without tying them into neat packages. Acu-Key 9 knits up the loose ends, showing you where, when, and what to do, to make you—in a word—all-powerful.

Together, as soon as I have elucidated a couple of final points for you, we are going to take the separate pieces of the Acupineology jigsaw puzzle which I have already spread before you, and click those pieces into a composite, logical whole.

The resulting picture will show you as the center piece, standing proud, far beyond previous woes and pain, rich in material and spiritual possessions, stepping unafraid into a glorious future.

Right now, I'm perfectly well aware that this sounds too good to be true. Perhaps you've read other books that promised the same, or more, and you've tried them and found yourself still snared by the same old hassles. You may still be scraping a living from day to day, fighting off creditors, and seeing each gray dawn in misery and hopelessness.

Let Acupineology change all that for you. I know it can, and I know from firsthand experience. If you've read my books, or followed my career since the late 60s, you're seeing a living example of these techniques working the way they should.

You may be aware that I've spent decades researching psychic and metaphysical matters. I've been up many blind alleys, found and discarded methods which lack value or credibility, and I've

Using Surplus Energy From Other People

investigated the claims of dozens of practitioners of the occult and psychic arts, crafts, and sciences.

The first breakthrough came in the early 70s. I was combining psychic research with a regular job to pay the rent and raise a family, when I evolved the first of my psychic methods which have made thousands of people contented, rich, and happy.

I know this to be true: I have their letters on file, attesting to it. I described that method in an earlier book. The Miracle of New Avatar Power. In the meantime, I began refining the techniques.

VcToria Comments: *I re-published The Miracle of New Avatar Power in April 2019. It can be purchased from my web store on my website* **www.alternativeuniverse.ca** *or Amazon. It is also available now in a Kindle edition.*

Within a few months, even before the book had been printed, I started climbing. I have not stopped since.

In the intervening years, during which I've been able to do as I please with no boss to tell me what to do, I've uncovered more jewels of forgotten techniques. And here they are, polished to a brilliance and sparkle, to help you grow mentally, spiritually, and materially.

Doubtful aspects of older methods of self-help have been abandoned. The result is Acupineology, the new science of using the free energy of your Creator to bring all you've ever dreamed about.

VcToria Comments: *As I have commented in the previous books that I have re-published all that my Dad wrote about in rising to the top after he* *connected to his psychic work is true. You only have to Google his name on the internet to know this. I was actually in the front room when he fell into a trance and summoned up one of his many guides through a process of 'automatic writing.' This complete story will be in a book that will be published by mid-2021.*

Please know that I use my extensive Numerology knowledge to create and add to my already fabulous life.

SOLAR SYSTEMIC NODES MAKE YOU THE BIG WINNER

One flaw in many methods of esoteric, metaphysical, psychic, or occult self-help is that the inventors imply that results come instantaneously.

I freely admit, in my earlier enthusiasm, I was as guilty of that error as anyone else.

I have now reached the firm conclusion that if any technique exists which works infallibly on any day of the year, the inventor is keeping it very quiet.

These techniques wax and wane as constantly as the moon in its phases. There are times when they are less effective for a while, just as a seed lies germinating in the earth at certain times of the year, to come bursting out later in full bloom.

Count the rings on a tree stump and you'll see that the tree grows faster in summer than in winter. That, in fact, is what causes the visible rings. If a tree grew steadily all year round, a stump would be as featureless as a slice of banana.

Just as seeds and trees obey the ebb and flow of natural energies, so then do your self-help methods, and Acupineology is no exception to that natural law.

Astrology lore

Here I can add the results of astrological research, which has been part of my path for a number of years now, resulting in much TV exposure and other profitable contacts.

I have confirmed, as astrologers have been saying for centuries, that a human being exists in tune with the movements of planets, and anyone's life can be interpreted by knowing his or her birth date.

I have also discovered that Acupineology works best for a person at key periods which can easily be established from the person's date of birth.

There is no need, however, for you to master the intricate art of astrology, with its intermingled analyses of the movements of eight planets and the Sun and Moon.

Here is a one-step method of discovering your *solar systemic nodes*, times when the world is your oyster, and iso-bionic energy will boost you to whatever heights you may envision.

This will be easiest for you if you obtain a calendar for the year, preferably one which has the 12 months all on one sheet.

If you have a wall calendar with a month on each page, you'll often find the whole year printed on the back of it. This is not absolutely necessary—it merely simplifies some easy counting you're about to carry out.

Using Surplus Energy From Other People

Your birthday

Find your birthday on the calendar and draw a ring around it with a pencil.

A special case will involve those of you who were born on February 29, as was the composer Rossini in 1792, or Pepper Martin, the baseball player, or Michele Morgan, that lovely French leading lady of the 30s and 40s.

If you share your birthday with these people, and you're using a calendar with a regular 365-day year, you should draw a ring around March 1. The reason for this is that you were born the day after February 28, which is February 29 in a leap year, and March 1 in other years.

Having circled your birthday, start counting through the year, a day at a time. Call the day after your birthday 1, the next day 2, then 3, and so on, until you reach 61, the sixty-first day after your birthday. Mark that date with a check mark, and start counting from 1 again, as you did from your birthday. When you reach 30, mark it with a small cross.

Start the count again from 1, and when you reach 31, mark the date with a check mark. A new count begins from there, up to 62, making a second cross at the date you have now reached.

Repeat the counting as before, up to 60. The date you arrive at should be marked with a check mark.

Starting at 1 again, count the days up to 31. That date is given a cross. Your final count begins, and when you reach 30, give that date a check mark.

VcToria Comments: *Just in case there is confusion here, you simply keep counting forward from each post where you were instructed to mark a check, cross and ring. Once reaching December 31st of your calendar go BACK to the same year on January 1st and continue counting forward.*

Eight solar systemic nodes

You now have a calendar with four check marks, three crosses, and a ring around your birth date.

Unless you were born in January, February, or very early in March, somewhere during the sequential counting routine you reached December 31. When that occurs, you merely return to the beginning of the calendar, to January 1, continuing your count without a break. January 1 does indeed follow December 31, and the fact that you're counting from the start of the same calendar year does not affect the outcome.

If you can, use a calendar which is not for a leap year. If it does include February 29, skip over that date when you reach it in your counting (unless February 29 is your birthday, in which case it becomes the starting point for your count).

The checked and crossed dates are your *solar systemic nodes*. The check-marked dates and the day before and the day after each one, is when your iso-bionic energy is at its highest, most positive, and constructive peak. Everything goes right when you work with Acupineology techniques during those periods.

Using Surplus Energy From Other People

The dates with crosses, and the day before and the day after each one, are your lower power periods. These are the times of the year when you're likely to experience obstacles against anything you attempt. Even Acupineology may not fully come up to expectations during these periods.

We can call the check-marked dates your "up" periods, and the cross-marked times your "down" periods.

Your birthday is a date on which you will have to experiment to see if it's an "up" or a "down" time. Some people find that the eve of their birthday, the day itself, and the following day are incredibly good times. Others say the opposite, finding that period to be unprogressive for them.

You can establish that for yourself by arranging an Acupineology routine on your birthday, or 24 hours on either side of it.

If the technique comes to glorious fruition, you can add your birthday to your check-marked "up" periods. If the experiment is not as successful as you would wish, add your birthday to the cross-marked "down" list, and avoid those periods when you're setting up Acupineology to bring major rewards.

The dates hold true for every year of your life. You can record your dates for use at any time in the future.

In between the "up" and the "down" periods, the tides of iso-bionic energy ebb and flow at an average level. As you approach an "up" period, your powers will usually be enhanced, while they can diminish in power as a "down" date approaches.

Using Surplus Energy From Other People

These are the solar systemic nodes which I have been mentioning at various stages of this work, thus filling in another piece of the jigsaw puzzle for you.

**TURN THE PAGE
TO START YOUR MIRACLE-WORKING**

You are now ready to read Acu-Key 9. These concluding pages will provide the keys to open the myriad doors I've shown you in preceding pages.

Proceed now to protect yourself against anything fate can send your way, and begin drawing toward yourself every last thing you've ever dreamed about—plus a few more for good measure.

Your Acupineology program awaits your pleasure!

Your Custom-Crafted Program of Towering Success

This is the time when we will put it all together as I promised, and you will receive your personal Acupineology program which can assuredly propel you upward and forward into joyful areas of experience which you may have trouble even considering right now.

Overall, your program is two-pronged. One part consists of regular, daily routines which are used to keep your iso-bionic energy at the highest possible peaks, so that you can gain the greatest benefits from your "up" solar systemic nodes, and to help counteract the less vital "down" nodes.

The second part of your program involves making use of your iso-bionic energy as and when you wish, being especially busy at your "up" times, of course.

NOTE YOUR SOLAR SYSTEMIC NODE PERIODS

Step one in your program needs to be performed only once. Carry out the calendar counting procedure described in Acu-Key 8, and mark your solar systemic nodes.

Make a note of your three-day "up" and "down" periods, plus a reminder to yourself to check on

Your Custom-Crafted Program of Towering Success

whether your birthday is an "up" or a "down," as I explained.

As you now know, your "up" periods are the very best times in the year to reach out for success. That does not imply that iso-bionic energy goes to sleep on you the rest of the time. The nodes are established from recognized astrological data, and besides the ones we have found, literally hundreds of other "up" periods occur for you. I have to omit them in these pages because they are different for everyone, being calculated individually from the time, date, and year of birth.

VcToria Comments: *You may choose, if you wish, to view my website store as I offer different astrology charts from a full natal and transit too many others that offer "lucky" times and also the year ahead for other "up" times. You will need an EXACT time of birth to order these.*

So, carry out your Acupineology techniques year round. Aim for major targets, where feasible, during your "up" periods, and avoid starting out for new life miracles during the three or four "down" periods you have identified.

VIBRATION NUMBER OF THE DAY

As described in Acu-Key 7, find the vibration number of the day before you begin your daily workout.

You'll notice a quick short-cut, once you've been finding these vibration numbers a few times. When you know the vibration number on one day, the following day's number is one higher than the previous day. The vibration numbers follow an increasing sequence, counting from 1 to 9, and then returning to 1 again.

So if, for instance, Thursday is a 4 day, Friday is 5, Saturday is 6, and so on, until you reach next Tuesday, which is 9. After that you return to 1: Wednesday will be a 1 day, and the sequence begins again from day to day as before.

That holds true as long as you do not move into a new month. Sunday, June 30, 2019, is a 3 day. Monday, July 1, 2019, is *not* a 3 day. The new month brings a new sequence into being. July 1, 2019, is a 2 day, and the counting goes on from there.

Check my figures for practice. You'll then fully understand what I mean, and you'll be able to check the vibration numbers carefully whenever a new month begins. Only in a non-leap year, as you move from February to March, is the sequence not broken.

VcToria Comments: *I have brought the dates into the time frame of the re-publishing of the book. The original book used earlier dates, but mine are mathematical correct as I too work in the same areas that my Dad did.*

TONES FOR THE DAY

Having found the vibration number for the day, note (from Acu-Key 7) the corresponding alpha-, beta-, and sigma-tone letters to be used with your iso-bionic energy field charging.

Example: The date is Sunday, June 30, 2019. The vibration number of that date is 3. Your alpha-tone is therefore C, your beta-tone is U, and your sigma-tone is L.

YOUR DAILY ACUPINEOLOGY WORKOUT

Your vital iso-bionic energy field charging takes about ten minutes each day. Try to schedule it within the routine of your daily life, just as you include time for eating, washing, sleeping, and any other basic features of living.

First, carry out the finger tip sensitizing routine described in Acu-Key 2. That takes about 80 seconds, or a minute and a half at the most.

Now, perform the umbilical, pectoral, and psinic gestures described in Acu-Key 1. Remember, you need only breathe deeply as you begin the exercise, there being no need to repeat the five breaths again. The total time taken should be about six and a half minutes.

Finally, as advised in Acu-Key 1, create your psinic vibration, then your pectoral swell, followed by your umbilical resonance, incorporating the appropriate tones in each, as explained in Acu-Key 7. You should be able to complete the triple repetition of the three sounds in roughly two minutes.

That's it. In ten minutes or less, your iso-bionic energy fields are raised to a foaming, coruscating peak, ready to do your bidding.

TURNING YOUR LIFE AROUND

The remainder of your Acupineology techniques can be divided into those which further increase available iso-bionic energy, and are used on an opportunity basis as and when circumstances occur to employ them, and those which are unerringly aimed at bringing specific miracles into your life.

OPPORTUNITIES FOR ISO-BIONIC ENERGY BOOSTS

Your umbilical, pectoral, and psinic gestures (Acu-Key 1), aside from being used regularly in your daily Acupineology workout, can also be made whenever you feel the need to top up your fields. It's impossible to overcharge them. Any surplus energy you generate will radiate to anyone else in your vicinity who needs it, thus spreading your bounty far and wide.

You can also perform the outdoor method of charging (Acu-Key 1) when the opportunity presents itself.

Your iso-bionic tideway is another "opportunity" technique, described in Acu-Key 8, where you will also find out when to apply it. And remember to practice drawing iso-bionic energy from anyone who shakes your hand, as is also described in Acu-Key 8.

SPECIFIC MIRACLES

Using iso-bionic energy for specific miracles is a multilevel program. You put things right in all spheres of your life, calming and shaping your mental processes, easing any physical discomfort, and changing your environment to conditions which give you the desired freedom, happiness, and fulfillment.

Your Custom-Crafted Program of Towering Success

You exist as a trinity of physical, mental, and spiritual levels. All three levels need to be in harmony with natural energy flows in order to achieve ultimate harmony.

Physical health (pectoral field)

Health is high on the list of desirable harmonies. Schedule the Jupiter connection, described in Acu-Key 3, to bring you maximum vitality. Although you will gain the greatest benefit from this technique when it is used as described at your "up" solar systemic node periods, you can perform the connection before sleeping on any day or night, especially if your health is at a low ebb.

If impotence or frigidity is a problem, Acu-Key 4 describes the necessary pollex massage. Use it daily, as and when convenient, until the condition is alleviated.

The pollex pressure point (Acu-Key 4) is also a valuable part of your program for feeling at ease. Use it exactly as described.

Mental harmony (psinic field)

Banishing fear and phobias with the pollex contact (Acu-Key 4) is ideal if you are uncertain, worried, stressed, or in any way less calm than you would wish.

As suggested, schedule a spare minute daily to dispel any mental disharmony, and add about 40 seconds of Moon massage (Acu-Key 5) to further increase your decisiveness and peace of mind.

The Moon barrier (Acu-Key 5) and the Moon defense (Acu-Key 6) represent powerful protective

Your Custom-Crafted Program of Towering Success

ploys, and will increase your self-confidence and impregnability.

Spiritual growth (umbilical field)

Acu-Key 6 describes some wonderful paths to peace. The concepts, abstract and working at inner levels, bring harmony to your soul, which quickly spreads to your mental and physical being.

The specific applications of astral travel which lead to akashic awareness and reincarnation experiences can be totally awesome in their effects. It is most worthwhile to persevere with this splendid mind technique.

It's rather futile to try to expound in advance on the incredible benefits you may gain. This is truly something you have to experience firsthand.

Emotional harmony (psinic field)

In order to feel emotionally peaceful, you need to be able to control people's effects on you. The pollex techniques, described in Acu-Key 4, open a broad path toward that desirable end. Personal harassment vanishes when you use the pollex contact as described.

Acu-Key 5 presents Moon techniques which further smooth your way into the future. If you are puzzled and undirected, using Moon massage and keeping up with the opposition with Moon contact will tell you what's going on, and disclose confidential secrets to you.

Probe deeper and acquire greater confidence with the astral travel techniques explained in Acu-Key 6, and gain ultimate power over others with

Your Custom-Crafted Program of Towering Success

dream guiding and mind touching, also found in that section of this book.

Material expansion (pectoral field)

Acu-Key 3 gives you the digital activator method which stimulates your pectoral field with the help of Jupiter techniques.

When you are face to face with a person whose decision will radically affect your material life, you can call on the Jupiter gesture. To gain monetary aid from a person in a partnership, make the described Jupiter connection.

If you're into any kind of deal and wish to show maximum profit, Jupiter massage is the technique for you.

If you're hoping to win a lottery or other gamble, use the Jupiter connection described for increasing your winning chances. But read that section again carefully before you set out on that project.

Uncovering hidden treasure or finding something you've lost can be done with the Moon connection presented in Acu-Key 5.

THE ULTIMATE SECRET

One more deceptively simple concept will conclude this summary of your program. I've touched on this briefly a couple of times in preceding pages.

Here it is again. When I am asked what is the true, genuine, bottom line, ultimate secret of success with any kind of mind power self-help system, this is my reply.

Your Custom-Crafted Program of Towering Success

When working with any technique where you know the intended result, *pretend it has already taken place*. Do your utmost to feel that, instead of the desire being in your future, it has already happened and you're savoring it to the fullest.

If you have no clear idea of your actual aim, try to produce the emotions you wish to experience. For the length of time when you are practicing the technique, feel the happiness, contentment, joy, and excitement you're wishing to come your way.

Truly, if you can master that exercise of the mind, you're at once an adept at all natural energy work.

AN ACUPINEOLOGY NOTEBOOK

As you get more deeply involved in Acupineology, it is a good idea to keep a notebook to record your successes, the techniques being used, plus your solar systemic nodes and other useful details. You could also make note of the pages in this book which you need to consult frequently.

A few minutes spent in recording such details can pay dividends. As your notebook is filled up, you can watch how your aims are fulfilled. You can see which techniques work best for you and which are less successful. The human memory can be a fallible tool, but if you have things down in writing, you'll know for sure whether last week's windfall came from the Jupiter gesture or the Jupiter massage.

You can make notes for the future, reminding you to carry out some Acupineology technique at a particular time for some special purpose.

Your Custom-Crafted Program of Towering Success

VcToria Comments: *You can set cell phones for reminders or pop up calendars on your e-mail area.*

I have left this example of someone who practices Acupineology on a serious level. This is an original page from the book published in 1980.

Nick W.'s Notebook

The following is a copy of a page from an Acupincology practitioner, Nick W., to illustrate how you might begin your notebook.

My "up" solar systemic nodes are March 7-9; May 6-8; July 6-8 September 5-7; November 5-7.

My "down" nodes are January 6-8; April 6-8; October 5-7.

Gambling works best for me on days having number 8 vibration. Number 3 days seem to go better in personal relationships.

Received raise on a 4 day; tax refund check arrived on 4 day; granted loan on 4 day. Keep watch on further money dealings—number 4 days look good.

Birthday of boss on April 4. Work out his "down" times, and check if he's snarkier than usual.

Nick's notes are comprehensive, but personal, so I've omitted references to sensitive areas of his life that he does not want exposed.

I find keeping notes to be very useful. These are not only notes about me and my life. I keep records of my wife's solar systemic nodes and those of several other important people in my life.

Your Custom-Crafted Program of Towering Success

Knowing the state of their energy patterns, whether they use iso-bionic energy knowingly or not, is valuable in all kinds of social and commercial intercourse.

ACUPINEOLOGY USES ONLY HOLY, CREATIVE ENERGY

To repeat a point I made much earlier, Acupineology is a science, a budding science, with many more facets to investigate, and which you will be uncovering to your total delight as you progress.

This is a science using natural energy, just as a tree uses natural energy to grow. The power you are using, named iso-bionic energy, is a creative, constructive, healing force, naturally available to all during this adventure of existence which we call life on earth.

Nowhere within the scheme of Acupineology are there any particularly mystical concepts, other than the mysteries of life in inner planes to which our Creator alone holds the full answers.

With little mysticism, Acupineology is pure and logical. Some self-help schemes introduce concepts which are suspect, and some people have quite correctly wondered whether some of the psychic techniques recently exposed may be less positive than they should be.

Yes, Acupineology does offer you the chance to roam in unseen planes, to draw strength and guidance from ancient energy patterns and apparent intelligences there. But, as the bedrock to such metaphysical exploration, you have the reassurance that iso-bionic energy leads you along ethical and progressive paths, far removed from any suspicion of diabolic powers, hellborn cults, or abysmal regions.

In brief, iso-bionic energy is as neutral and helpful as the electricity which lights your home, or the sunshine which warms you in summer.

BE GENEROUS
WITH YOUR NEW-FOUND POWERS

The system I have offered you is designed to help you toward happiness, health, and wealth. I suggest that your first priority should be acquiring whatever you need with the aid of iso-bionic energy to reach your own heaven on earth.

Once you've climbed to that pinnacle, you can start to spread your new-found powers around, to help the less fortunate whom you left whimpering behind you as you soared ahead to glory.

The methods for passing on your bounty are currently being researched, confirmed, and organized. You, as an early practitioner of this young and burgeoning science of Acupineology, can carry out your own research, to your own ultimate benefit.

The day may dawn when the title of Registered Acupineologist is recognized, along with the other helping professions.

With that day still in the future at the time of this writing, you could be at the forefront of this new wave of natural energy application. As a pioneer, your usage of iso-bionic energy could bring you admiration, fame, and reverence.

VcToria Comments: *Depending on when you have purchased this book, will depend on whether I* *have created courses yet. My intention is to create courses and on-line courses. Please keep an eye on my monthly newsletter for updates on this. My monthly newsletter can be found on my website.*

Current researchers with whom I am acquainted have established several basic tenets of iso-bionic energy.

When transmitting the energy to another person, it works best if the two people, the transmitter and the receiver, are in physical contact.

The various mounts and planetary fingers have a distinct bearing on the objective of any experiment. Iso-bionic energy, in face-to-face situations, often seems to flow *from* the right hand and *to* the left hand and psinic, pectoral, and umbilical focuses.

For instance, to promote general healing and to complement orthodox medical treatments, the Acupineologist massages the tip of his or her Jupiter finger of their right hand onto the Sun mount of the patient's left hand. The concept behind that technique is that the abundance of the Jupiter finger feeds energy into the health area connected with the Sun.

Considerable success has been reported in treating impotence, premature ejaculation, and frigidity, using pollex techniques. This entails intimate massage and pressures, and I recommend that you try this, as previously advised, only with people who are fully aware of what you are doing, who know the object of the exercise, and who will not later take offense and cause you problems.

A right Saturn finger massaging another person's mount of Neptune on their left hand seems

Your Custom-Crafted Program of Towering Success

to stabilize and eradicate confusion of mind, while the same finger applied to the mount of the Moon calms hysteria to a marked extent.

If you scan the subjects in Figure 2, you will no doubt be able to evolve your own routines to dispel undesirable conditions.

I must add a final disclaimer to this section; otherwise, I would be derelict in my duties to both you and myself.

This book is written as a *self-help method*, designed to enable you to use your own iso-bionic energy to gain freedom from want. Any cooperative work with a third party, or any suggestions I have made to work in contact with someone else, are speculative and I cannot accept any responsibility whatsoever for any results or lack of results from such involvements.

Clearly, iso-bionic energy will help you to help yourself. Whether it will help you to help other people is open to further research and conjecture.

TRANSFORMING DISCOMFORT TO DELIGHT IS ACUPINEOLOGY'S PRIME OBJECTIVE

Although I have previously touched lightly on this aspect of Acupineology, I'd like to reinforce the thought as this book draws to a close.

Acupineology employs natural energies to transport you from frustrating conditions to situations where you are safe from harm, peaceful, and fulfilled.

The point I wish to emphasize is that iso-bionic energy will carry you along the most direct path to

Your Custom-Crafted Program of Towering Success

happiness, ensuring that your desired peace of mind comes as efficiently as possible. You no doubt have your own firm ideas of what you need to make you happy. Be prepared to modify your notions if iso-bionic energy offers you a different path.

In this existence, you have the God-given facility of free will. You can take any action you please, provided you're prepared to accept the consequences of your deliberate actions. Acupineology may clearly show you that your next step toward happiness is to accept a certain set of circumstances. You, however, may have different plans, and if you choose to go your way, iso-bionic energy will neutrally step aside and allow your free will to operate.

So, when iso-bionic energy brings change, it may not be the change you were expecting. If conflict seems to exist between Acupineology's urgings and your aspirations, take time out to consider what is going on.

You'll almost certainly find, in the long run, that iso-bionic energy is suggesting the correct path for stable self-fulfillment. The whole idea of Acupineology is to make you permanently happy and content, not temporarily stimulated and then dropped back to the same slough you were in before.

Point made. Think it over. Later, you'll see what I am driving at.

PERFECTION BECKONS, SO SAVOR IT TO THE FULLEST

We have now reached the end of this book, an end which promises to be a new beginning for you.

Your Custom-Crafted Program of Towering Success

I have done my best to hand over to you my understandings of Acupineology. Now it's your turn to use the techniques and methods to climb out of the rut of frustration and restriction to the mountain peak of freedom and joy.

However much you may believe the contrary, no matter how depressing the newspaper headlines may be, there is enough peace, joy, and happiness on this planet for everyone to have their share, with plenty left over for generations to come.

Harmony and freedom from want can be achieved, even from the most desperate circumstances.

You now have the guidelines for attaining your share of the good things. You are about to become, if you wish, a fully operational and successful Acupineologist. Once you have seen iso-bionic energy doing its wonderful work for you, I know you'll never be quite the same person again.

Reach out. May Acupineology bring your every desire to glittering reality, and may you be fully enthralled by them in the days, months, and years of your destined future.

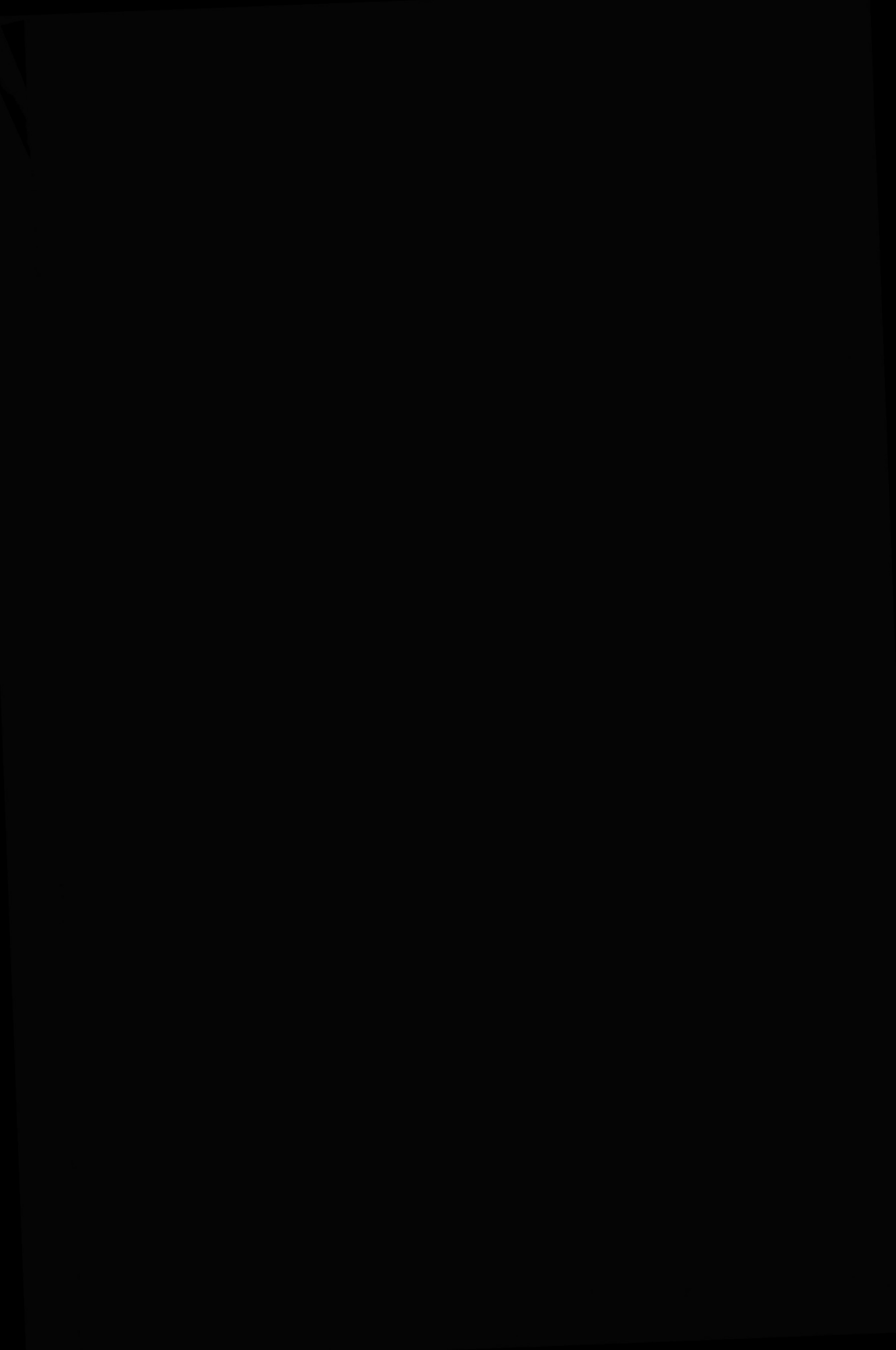

www.ingramcontent.com/pod-product-compliance
Lightning Source LLC
Chambersburg PA
CBHW072007070526
44583CB00015B/1368